Walking
in the
Cotswolds
with Sue Gearing

Cotswold Walks

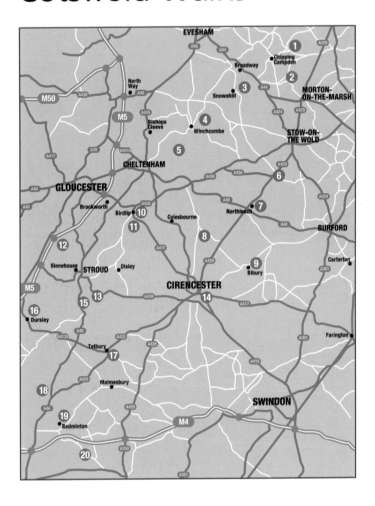

Discovering the "mouse man"

Mickleton – Hidcote Manor – Ilmington – Hidcote Manor – Mickleton
About 8 miles, 4 hours walking or 5 miles, 2.5 hours walking

OS Explorer map 205, Stratford upon Avon and Evesham.

Longer walk start Mickleton: Ref 161 434

Shorter walk, start Hidcote Manor: 177 429

In the beautiful church at Ilmington, we encounter "the mouse man of Kilburn", a great woodcarver whose signature was a small carved mouse. It's just one of several pleasant discoveries on this circle of exploration on the very northern edge of the Cotswolds. There is a choice of lengths, and it would be worth doing at different times of the year. In winter it will be very peaceful as some attractions won't be open. In summer when the area is clothed in green you will encounter more people and you can take advantage of the various open gardens, maze and tearooms. Hidcote Manor Garden is the highlight of this circle. Added to this is another beautiful garden, Kiftsgate Court, and a fascinating summer–time maze in a field of maize just by Hidcote (open until September). Walking is on good footpaths and quiet lanes up on the escarpment and also for a short while along the edge of the Vale of Evesham. In Ilmington there is a choice of pubs. It's a memorable, challenging walk with some steep hills.

START Long route begins at Mickleton village on the B4632 about 25 miles north of Chipping Campden and about 6 miles east of Evesham. Short route begins at the car park for Hidcote Manor. Turn off the main road and park near the church.

1 Church Keeping the church on your left take the footpath straight ahead through a hunting gate at the side of a large wooden gate. Head straight across just to the left of a large oak through a metal kissing gate, and then continue in the same direction up the next field. Cross a stile by more oak trees and now carry on up the path which bends and goes up the centre of the field through the full length of the field. It narrows to a gap between hedges. Go through and take the path more steeply uphill following the blue arrow to the top left corner by the wall and lodge house of Kiftsgate Court.

2 Kiftsgate Court Leave by the blue wicket gate onto a lane. Over by the left is Kiftsgate Court Gardens, open to the public, selling unusual plants and serving lunches and teas. The beautiful interconnecting gardens, famous for their roses, were created by women gardeners and begun in 1920. No dogs are allowed in the gardens.

Go straight ahead up the lane and if you are coming in summer you will soon reach the Maize Maze on your left.

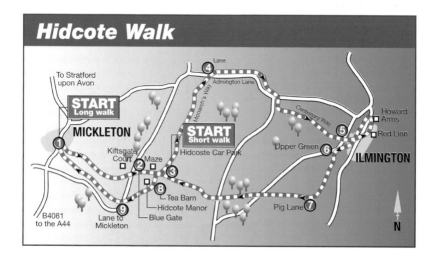

This summer fun activity takes place in about 8 acres planted out each year to a different maze pattern. Continue on to reach Hidcote Gardens car park.

The Short Walk begins at Hidcote. Park in the car park if it is open and you can visit Hidcote itself afterwards. In winter when the car park is closed, find somewhere suitable nearby to park.

❸ Hidcote car park
BOTH ROUTES: Go through the car park and take the marked public footpath on the left through a seven bar gate. Follow the arrow diagonally across the field heading for the corner hedge which juts into the field. Then keep ahead along the left hedge and across a stile at the end. Carry on a little way but before climbing onto the ridge, drop left downhill down a gully/small valley following the arrow. About 150 yards from the foot, turn right along the contour of the hill, over a stile and through woodland. Continue on above the valley bottom through another field, and over a stile and through more woodland to reach another field.

Stay fairly close to the trees on the left and a stream which is rather well hidden and just continue through the fields all

© Clint Hughes

the way to the far tip of the last field, passing under power lines on route. Here cross left over a footbridge and stile and then go right along to a lane.

❹ **Lane** Turn right and follow this quiet lane for nearly a mile through the edge of the Vale of Evesham, going round a couple of bends and ignoring a left turning. Just past Lark Stoke Cottage turn right on a small lane. It starts to rise and at a triangle of grass turn left on the Centenary Way on a good dry drive/track.

Go through the hunting gate at the side of larger gates and follow the path downhill keeping the fence on your right. Bend left on the path and come to a pond. Before you reach it, go right over two stiles and continue on the path, which starts to climb gently and then follow along the top fence. Cross a stile and carry on in the same direction with the hedge on your right. It will not be far before you come to a stile on the right. Cross over and walk diagonally across the field, dropping down with a pond on your left, through a band of willow trees, and then up to the top fence line to find a marked stile. Follow the footpath arrows diagonally across the centre. On the far side ignore the Centenary Way ahead and instead go to the left on a

© Clint Hughes

wide grassy track which bends down into the village of Ilmington. Don't go straight out by the cottages – instead follow the footpath arrow left through a gate into a stable yard and take the path which bends round and comes down to the village road.

❺ **Ilmington** Go right a few yards and then left down the tarmac church path under a line of twelve lime trees, representing the twelve apostles.

The woodwork in the church is remarkable as one of the finest examples of the work of Robert Thomson "the mouseman" of Kilburn, Yorkshire whose signature on his work was a small carved mouse. Look for this little mouse on doors, desk, pulpit and pews and a memorial plaque to Spencer Flower.

We are going to take a small circuit of the village to see some of the pretty cottages and passing by two pubs. So, go left on

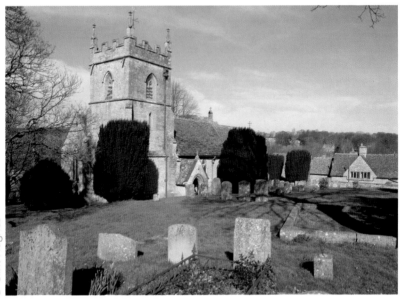

© Clint Hughes

the church path and follow it round left again. Then bend right (ahead in the field are the old fishponds if you want a quick visit) still the tarmac path coming to a beautiful thatched cottage at the end. Turn left on another tarmac path which is known as Middle Lane.

Half way down here, opposite a wicket gate on the left, go right up a narrow alley between cottages. Reach a road at the end and turn left to the Red Lion, a popular village pub selling a range of snacks and meals. Carry on past the Red Lion to the green, noting the village stocks over on the right, and at Lower Green reach the other inn, the Howard Arms. Turn left into Lower Green passing an interesting village information board and then take the small No Through Road (Middle Lane again) passing the post office and stores. Soon come back to where you turned off for the Red Lion and just continue up the lane alongside a small stream. At the end of Middle Lane by the thatched cottage you reached earlier, turn left and walk along the road. Turn right and right again along Front Street, past the site of the former village pound.

❻ Upper Green Stay along the bottom of Upper Green, surrounded by glorious cottages and passing the old village well/fountain. At the end of the green, go left and up Frog Lane past more pretty cottages. At the end of the Lane keep ahead on the footpath through a gate and pass the village allotments. Go through a kissing gate and keep straight ahead along a fenced path. Cross a stile and footbridge and ahead in a field with the right edge fairly close by and continue up into the next field and immediately go right over a marked footbridge and stile then left up the field in the same direction as before. Follow the left fence up this field and then next, climbing steadily uphill. Go over a stile at the top and then through a metal gate onto a track and look down onto Foxcote House, an impressive Georgian home.

❼ Pig Lane Turn right up the track. Go up through woodland and continue to climb up onto the ridge. Keep ahead for about half a mile to reach communication masts. Follow the track ahead down to a road. Turn left for a few yards and then right up a marked path up the right hedge to the top, ignoring a stile on the right. Go through a gate and band of woodland and keep on climbing until you reach more masts – about a third of a mile from the earlier masts.

Cross the track, go ahead on the RUPP, (Road used as a Public Path) with good views north over the Vale of Evesham and into the Welsh mountains. The track bends. Follow it all the way downhill back to Hidcote Manor Garden car park – a distance from the second masts of about a third of a mile. The thatched tea barn, plant shop and entrance to Hidcote are down on the left.

FOR THE LONGER ROUTE turn left at the lane, which is in fact putting you back on the Monarch's Way, and reach the tea barn.

❽ Hidcote tea bar Pass the entrance to Hidcote. Keep on, passing a small pond on the left and at the end go ahead for a few yards into raspberry fields following the footpath and turn right following the footpath arrow. On your right you can look into the gardens of Hidcote. Turn right through a wooden kissing gate into an orchard. Go ahead through the orchard fairly close to the right hedge

until after about 100 yards you come to a footpath post. Cross a kind of ditch and turn left along it (ignoring footpath arrows going on ahead). Pick up a track, which takes you along and into another field over a stile. Cross diagonally down the length to a stile in the far corner which leads onto a lane.

⑨ **Lane to Mickleton** Go down the lane marked to Mickleton for about a third of a mile. Go right on the marked public footpath to Mickleton down the field with woodland on your right. Cross over the fence on the left and just before the fence corner go left through a wooden kissing gate into a field. Go down the right fence to the bottom corner and then through into woodland. Follow the path through and out the other side into a field. Keep straight ahead along the left edge and go through a kissing gate and drop down to Mickleton Church. The church is worth a visit, and is noted for its beautiful range of kneelers.

Kiftsgate Court Gardens

opens 12am-6pm, June and July, Mon, Wed, Thurs, Saturday and Sunday; August – Sept, Wed, Thurs and Sundays 2-6pm.

Adults £5.00, children £1.50.
Light lunches and teas.
Tel: 01386 438777

Maize Maze opens
July 19 – September 7, 10am – 6pm,
Adults £3.75, children £2.75.
Tel: 01386 430178

Hidcote Manor Gardens as one of
England's great gardens, created by the
horticulturist Major Lawrence Johnston.
A series of outdoor rooms each with
a different character. The garden is
famous for its rare shrubs and trees,
outstanding herbaceous borders and
unusual plant species.
Hidcote is liable to overcrowding
on Bank Holiday Mondays and fine
Sundays.

Open: 19th March to 2nd Oct daily
except Thur & Fri 10.30am – 6.00pm
(but open Good Fri); 3rd Oct – 30th
Oct: daily except Thur & Fri. 10.30am –
5pm. Last admission 1hr before closing
or dusk if earlier.

Adults £6.00, Child £3.30;
a family £16.10. Groups: £5.90,
Child £2.65 Free car park.

There is a thatched tea bar and plant
shop outside the entrance open from
10:30am until 5pm until the end
of September serving light snacks and
drinks.

If you pay for entry there is also
a licensed garden restaurant and
National Trust Shop.

For information about Hidcote
Tel: 01386 438333

Red Lion, Ilmington
Tel: 01608 682 366
No food on Mondays, but open for drinks.

The Howard Arms, Ilmington
Tel: 01608 682 226
Serves food every lunchtime.

There's an old mill by the stream

Batsford – Blockley – Batsford

About 5 miles. 2.25 hours walking.

OS map Outdoor Leisure 45 the Cotswolds, ref: 169 332

This short ramble calls in at picturesque honey-coloured Blockley which hugs the side of a hill, followed by the chance to visit an old water mill garden which is beautiful all year round but particularly in Spring with thousands of tulips, daffodils, fritillaria and irises. As is usually the case in Cotswold combe country, there are two or three hills to negotiate. There is an outstanding inn tucked away in Blockley village and in season you can take lunch or tea at the gardens in Mill Dene. The circle passes through the tranquil estate village of Batsford Park which is now run as an arboretum, falconry and garden centre. Your dog will enjoy the walk but is not allowed in Mill Dene.

© Clint Hughes

START On a quiet lane running from Bourton-on-the-Hill to Batsford. On the extreme west end of Bourton, take the B4479 marked to Blockley and Paxford, then fork right towards Batsford and Aston Magna. After about half a mile, by a wall round woodland, park safely on the verge near the gate and footpath which crosses this road. It is signed as the Monarch's Way or Heart of England's Way. You will see the signpost most easily on the wall side of the road.

❶ Crossing footpath Take the marked footpath over a stile by a gate on the right (if coming from Bourton-on-the-Hill direction). It goes into woodland and you are asked to keep dogs on leads. Follow this along a mossy Cotswold stone wall (on the left) on the flat and then downhill, where you get views over Batsford Park on the left. Reach a track by the gate into Parkland. Turn right and at the junction of tracks, turn left, still gently ascending. Good pastoral views unfold along here. At a left bend in the track, fork right on the marked path which goes down to a stile. Cross and

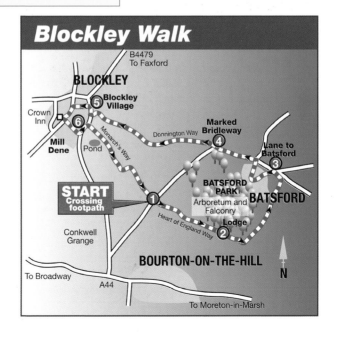

Blockley Walk

go straight down the field, through a gate to a crossing drive which leads to Batsford Park. The house and grounds date from the 17th Century and were much altered and extended over the years. Towards the last quarter of the 19th Century the estate was inherited by Algernon Redesdale (later Lord Redesdale). He had been influenced by his travels in China and Japan and was fascinated by the plants there, especially bamboos. After rebuilding the mansion, he turned his attention to the gardens and developed radical new plans, combining conventional parkland with a garden landscape. Most of the major trees were his original plantings. He also created one of the foremost bamboo collections of the time. The estate was sold in 1919 to Gilbert Alan Hamilton Wills, later the 1st Lord Dulverton. Quite a number of the larger trees were planted during this time, most notably maples, pines, redwoods, spruces and firs. The garden was developed by Frederick Wills who became 2nd Lord Dulverton and raised the status of Batsford to an arboretum of international standing. The Batsford Arboretum is run by a charity, the Batsford Foundation. In 2002 the Arboretum was recognised as holding the national collection of Japanese Village Cherries. Nowadays there is a garden centre, tearoom and other attractions for families.

❷ **Lodge** Go straight across the drive and through the marked gate ahead to the right of the lodge house. This field may be rather muddy so pick your route! Go over to the left wall and follow it along until you reach a crossing footpath. Turn left through the gate and follow the hedge through several fields with hedge or wall to your left. Soon you can see Batsford Park house on the left and more of the parkland. You carry on to join a footpath still in the same direction with the ranch facing your left and follow this all the way to a road. Turn left and very shortly turn left again.

❸ **Lane to Batsford** This is a no through lane to Batsford hamlet which takes you under a magnificent avenue of limetrees. At the junction, our way continues by going right, but you may like to go ahead for a short distance to the church. Follow the lane along with the estate houses and buildings of the Batsford Stud on your left and reach the road briefly earlier. Turn left on the quiet road marked to Blockley (25 miles). It is now a gentle ascent, and you pass over on the left just in front of the stables a "horse carousel" where I was intrigued to see several magnificent horses exercising.

❹ **Marked bridleway** At the top of the hill and a bend, leave the road and go

straight ahead on the marked bridleway through a gate.

Go down to the bottom left corner with great views ahead across the valley. Go through and continue along the right hedge in the next field, walking along the edge of the hill.

There is a crossing path and two paths going ahead when you reach the end. Take the right hand of the two gates ahead and it is the furthest away. Come into a field and go ahead, still along the edge of the hill and here enjoy pretty views across to Blockley. Keep on following arrows and you will see that you are now following Donnington Way.

Start to drop downhill, you will soon see a large modern barn in the direction you are heading. Go to the left of the barn and pick up a track which heads downhill to the village and reaches the road. Turn right into Blockley.

⑤ Blockley Village This picturesque village tucked into a Cotswold fold flourished in the 18th and 19th Centuries as a silk-working centre supplying silk thread to the ribbon trade.

After a few minutes, just before a bend, when you are about opposite the church

which you can see up above on the left, look for a tarmac path on the left climbing up at the side of a stone garage with arched door which is set back from the road. At the top go left through to the church. St Peter and St Paul's church welcomes visitors but asks walkers to remove muddy boots. It is a light and airy church which for more than a thousand years has been a landmark at the centre on Blockley. From the church door, turn left and go up the village street. Keep straight ahead passing the old stone cottages and going onto the raised pavement which brings you along to the Crown, a beautifully managed pub with delicious snacks and meals and very friendly staff. Our muddy dog was even allowed in!

Continue on a couple of houses past The Crown, and take a tarmac path left downhill, reaching Mill House at the bottom and turn left with the Blockley Brook on your right. This is a very beautiful quiet area of the village. Ignore the no through road on the left and continue to a bend with Mill Dene of the left.

⑥ Mill Dene Wendy Dare and her husband have transformed over 25 acres of land around their stone watermill home into an all-year-round garden made up of a series of "rooms" displaying different colours of flowers and foliage at their best in different seasons. Sited in its own steep sided valley, the garden had hidden paths winding up from the mill-pool and stream at the bottom through the Rose Walk to the Cricket Lawn.

Turn left from Mill Dene and come up to the main road. Turn left and cross over on to a path (The Quiet Lanes Path) up on the bank, which goes alongside the main road and has a special non-slip surface. Reach a marked footpath on the right up a track – the Monarch's Way and Heart of England Way.

The Monarch's way extends for 610 miles between Worcester to Shoreham in Sussex following the route taken by Charles II when he escaped to France after the Battle of Worcester in 1851. The Heart of England Way is a 100 mile route from Stafford to Burton-on-the-Water.

The track takes you over a stile into a field. Follow the arrows ahead with the hedge on the left. Go over another stile at the side of a gate and climb up the field. Go over a crossing track and come up to a stile. Cross and follow the arrow up the hill, staying over towards the left hand side of the field (ignoring sheep tracks) to leave the field in the top left corner. Take your time as you climb uphill and look back

Cross the stile at the top and go left on the path. After going through a gate across the track, immediately turn right on the Monarch's Way into a field and go up the right hedge. Continue on into another field with the wall to your right, leaving through the metal gate at the end. Follow a short piece of track which brings you to the lane where you started.

The Crown Inn, Blockley
Tel: 01386 700245

Mill Dene is open from April 1 to October. www.milldene.co.uk.
Tel: 01386 700457
Admission adult £4.50, Children under 15 £1.00 and senior £4.00.

Completely Cotswold

Snowshill – Laverton – Stanton – Snowshill

6.2 miles. 3 hours walking.

OS Outdoor Leisure Map 45, The Cotswolds, ref: 097 340

From the grandeur of Snowshill
Manor this circle heads out across
the hills and combes the heart
of Cotswold country to Laverton
Village and then to the beauty of
Stanton where a hillside pub with
good views awaits your pleasure.
True, it is a 15 minute climb shortly

after Stanton, but then it's along Shenberrow Hill, and a drop down
through woods and fields back to the pretty village of Snowshill.

Image above and opposite © Clint Hughes

START in the free public car park just outside Snowshill village, next to the Snowshill Manor National Trust car park (which is only for members). Snowshill lies about 25 miles south of Broadway and can easily be reached from the B4077, Evesham – Stow Road.

1 Snowshill car park Turn left on the lane at the top of the entrance drive to Snowshill Manor, go right over a marked stile and immediately your walk starts with

good Cotswold views and peace. Follow the arrow down the field, through a kissing gate and carry on down. Through another one and immediately turn left and follow the fence along and down into the valley. Go through a gate into woodland. Follow the path which bends right in the woods (don't make the mistake of going into the field at this point). Leave the woods over a stile and follow the arrow along the left fence, climbing gently, again with tranquil views. Go through a metal kissing gate and right on a tarmac drive.

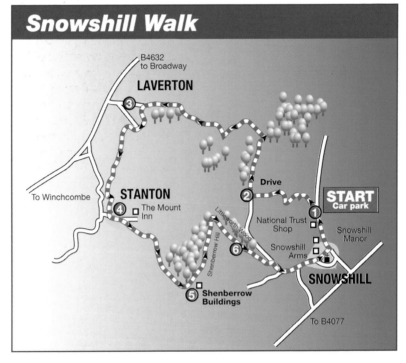

Snowshill Walk

B4632 to Broadway

LAVERTON

To Winchcombe

STANTON

The Mount Inn

Drive

START Car park

National Trust Shop

Snowshill Manor

Snowshill Arms

Shenberrow Hill

Littleworth Wood

Shenberrow Buildings

SNOWSHILL

To B4077

② **Drive** As you follow this there are great views on the right across to Snowshill Village on the hill. Bend left and go through a gate across the track and cross left over a marked stile into a field on the edge of the hill. Look across to Broadway Tower up on the hill in the distance. Go along the edge of the hill for a short distance and then bear away right across the field to a stile onto a farm track near the far right corner. This is the Cotswold Way. Turn left and ignore a stile on the right. Follow the track along until you go through a gate across the track. Just before woodland, turn right off the Cotswold way onto a stony bridleway which takes you all the way down the hill into the quiet hamlet of Laverton.

③ **Laverton** like its neighbours Buckland and Broadway, it sits on the edge of the Vale of Evesham just under the Cotswold escarpment. Turn left in the village and follow the lane along and round past the village hall and continue to bend round (almost going in a half circle). Just past a rather grand old house on the left, the last in the village, turn left over a stile on a public footpath. Follow the left fence and continue through the fields on the flat looking up at Shenberrow Hill up on the left until you approach a large equestrian centre where there will be horses grazing. Go through a double wooden squeeze

stile and get close to the stable building. Stay over to the left and cross a stile by a hunting gate and continue ahead passing the large stables and in the corner go over a waymarked stile. Go ahead in the field along the right edge and then turn right through a large iron kissing gate and follow the iron railings of the path along and round to Stanton church, which still has some Norman work evident and is well worth a visit.

Go out through the main gate and along the village street and turn left.

④ **Stanton** Nestling below Shenberrow Hill, Stanton is an idyllic Cotswolds village where little has changed in 300 years. It

has a picturesque long main street with several delightful corners. The houses are built in typical Cotswolds style with steeply pitched gables, mullioned windows and glowing honey coloured limestone walls. Reach the Cotswold Way sign going right in the village, but if you want refreshment make a short detour first going straight ahead for a few minutes up to the Mount Inn which has glorious views across the Vale of Evesham and to the Malverns.

Return to the Cotswold Way, and at the end by a magnificent thatched house follow the Cotswold Way left towards Buckland. The track gently climbs. Before reaching a gate across the track, follow the Cotswold Way sign right down through a hunting gate and through woodland and another gate. Continue on the path along the bottom of the field and through the trees for a few yards and then bed left uphill, starting to go up Shenberrow Hill. Continue all the way up the hill for about another 12 minutes, climbing quite steeply, following the waymark signs until you reach a farm, marked on the map as Shenberrow Buildings.

5 Shenberrow Buildings Follow the Cotswold Way to the left of the farm and over a stile into the field. Go straight ahead on the sandy track and across the top of Shenberrow Hill with great views

❼ Snowshill It's worth having a look around Snowshill. Follow the road out of the village to the car park and the entrance to the Manor, restaurant and shop. The gardens are particularly interesting, designed by Charles Paget Wade as a series of outdoor rooms and are a wonderful mixture of colours, architectural features, ornaments and scents.

The Mount Inn, Stanton
Tel: 01386 584316

The Snowshill Arms
Tel: 01386 852653

Snowshill Manor and Gardens,
open March to the end October, closed Mons and Tues.
For details Tel: 01386 852410
*Shop and restaurant are open weekends through November and December and during these two months non members are welcome.

depending on the weather. Go over a cattle grid and turn right on the tarmac track. Pass alongside Littleworth Wood on your left and a National Trust sign for the wood, go left through the kissing gate.

❻ Wood Follow the path through the wood, ignoring side turns. Leave by a stile bringing you into a field. Head diagonally across and down with glorious views across to Snowshill village. Go through a metal gate onto a tarmac farm track and turn right. Turn left at the junction and continue on to the next junction with a lane. Turn left again and follow the lane under trees downhill into Snowshill village.

Winchcombe wonder

Winchcombe – Sudeley Castle – Hailes Abbey – Greet – Winchcombe

About 9 miles. 4.5 hours walking.

Outdoor Leisure 45, The Cotswolds. ref 023 282

A Cotswolds 'tour de force'
taking in a castle, a ruined abbey,
a holy well, steam railway, a
small railway museum as well
as a stunning ancient Cotswold
town with beautiful cottages
and houses. Our walk circles
round Winchcombe through a
mixture of parkland and fields,
on footpaths and dry tracks
and takes in sections of several

long distance paths, the Windrush Way, the Warden's
Way, Gloucester Way and the Wychavon Way. The terrain
includes two or three hills, a couple of them reasonably
steep. Altogether it is a good up and down mix that makes
Cotswold walking so rewarding and interesting. There is
a good pub about three quarters of the way round in the
village of Greet.

START Go to beautiful **Winchcombe (the home of Sudeley Castle)** on the **B4632**, to the north east of Cheltenham. Park in the long stay car park behind the library (toilets here). It is clearly signposted.

①Car park Winchcombe was the capital of the old Saxon Kingdom of Mercia and is an interesting, beautiful town of narrow streets and much history. It is well worth further exploration.

Leave from the corner of the car park following the sign to the town centre, down Cowl Lane – so named because the Monks of Winchcombe Abbey walked the lane with their cowls covering their heads – joins the High Street, go left and immediately right on the Windrush Way down Castle Street.

Castle Street has been known by different names over the years – Birporte, Sudeley, Tanyard Bank – and it's one of Winchcombe's attractive features that street plaques explaining the town's history have been displayed. Cross the River Isbourne and reach Chandos Hall on the right. Take the Windrush Way

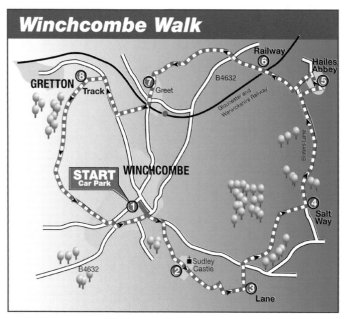

Winchcombe Walk

footpath at the side up steps and enter the parkland. Your general direction is across the park towards the castle paralleling the right edge and then make your way over to the left side to a waymarked wooden kissing gate under a large sycamore. Go through and turn right along the edge to come out onto the castle drive. Cross and take the hunting gate opposite at the side of a metal drive gate. Enter more parkland and keep close to the left boundary, passing a children's play area. Ignore a metal kissing gate on the left.

❷ **Castle** Just continue along the left fence through the beautiful parkland with good views and the castle on the left. Don't be lured to fork right on the Cotswold Way. Stay over to the left and at the fence corner, continue straight across the parkland always following the Warden's Way, the arrow marked with a large W.

Sudeley Castle is set in 1500 acres of hills and landscaped parkland and 900 years of history. Queen Elizabeth 1 was one of the castle's Royal visitors. Sudeley was also the home of Katherine Parr who had the distinction of outliving Henry VIII and, the castle also became a refuge for Charles 1.

Continue across parkland to the corner and cross a stile and immediately go left over a second stile, still on the Warden's Way. Continue with fence on left, going round the field corner and along until you reach a willow tree where there is a bridge on the left over the stream. Once over, climb up the field edge, with good views of the castle and come to a small lane.

❸ **Lane** Turn left on the lane, leaving the Wardens' Way. At the t-junction go left on the road and, after a few yards, at the entrance to Sudeley Hill Farm, take the footpath to the right. The path goes up the field, climbing reasonably steeply.

Go over stile in direction of the arrow, still climbing. Reach a stile and gate on the far side with a house on the right. Join a track and pass below the chapel-like 'conduit house' for St Kenelm's Well.

The well dates from Saxon times. It marks the spot where the body of Kenelm, king and martyr, 'rested' on its way to Winchcombe Abbey. In the reign of Queen Elizabeth 1, Lord Chandos of Sudeley enshrined the holy well by building the 'conduit' house you are now looking at, probably to mark one of Elizabeth's visits to Sudeley. The carving, of St Kenelm, was added in 1887 to mark the jubilee of Queen Victoria.

Continuing on, go over a stile by a gate

and turn right up the field, although the climb is steep it is well worth it for the amazing views over the castle. Up on the right is a large Cotswold stone barn. Head for the left corner of the stone wall running along the top of the field, with the barn on the right, standing sentinel over the valley. Climb the stone steps over the wall at the side of the gate and now continue up following the boundary all the way to the lane – Salt Way. Turn left.

❹ **Salt Way** Salt ways, such as this, were named after the transportation of salt by the merchants who with the aid of pack horses distributed this essential commodity throughout the country.

There are breathtaking views as you drop down the hill. Ignore all the side paths. Eventually leave the common area over a cattle grid and the Salt Way has now become Salter's Lane. Pass cottages in Hailes Green. Take the Cotswold Way on the right by one of the cottages. Follow the stony track to the end and through the gate, following the Cotswold Way ahead across the field and come out through a kissing gate to the left of Hailes Abbey to the lane.

❺ **Hailes Abbey** It is well worth visiting the atmospheric ruins of this 16th Century Cistercian abbey in the care of English Heritage. It was a pilgrimage site

in medieval times as it reputedly housed a vial of Christ's blood. There is a small museum on the site and cold drinks and ice creams are also on sale in the shop.

Across the road from the Abbey is the ancient small parish church renowned for its medieval wall paintings. Note also the well preserved box pew at the back.

If you want a snack or lunch to this point you could make a detour up the lane past the abbey to Hailes Fruit Farm, forking right down the drive. It has a farm shop and café.

To continue our circle go down the lane past the small church, keeping it on your right, and at the junction, turn left back on to the end of Salter's Lane. At the left bend, go straight ahead on the Cotswold Way. Before the hedges on each side of the track end, go right over a stile rather hidden in the hedge, but marked as a public footpath. Follow the left edge of

the field and just before the corner, go left over two stiles and take the path which goes under the Gloucestershire and Warwickshire Railway.

⑥ **Railway** This line which has been brought alive by enthusiastic volunteers has a unique collection of heritage diesel locomotives. If you happen to be here on one of their operating or gala days you may well see one of these wonderful old engines chuffing along the line.

Cross a stile by a gate and now follow the right hedge towards a farm. The hedge along here was a mass of red hawthorn berries when I came along here in September. Before reaching the farm, cross a stile on the right and then follow the hedge on your left, passing the farm and going out onto the road by the footpath sign.

Cross over into the field opposite and go round the left edge. Go left into another field and now go diagonally sharp right (or round the right edge if there are crops) to a marked stile and footbridge over a stream. Cross the field to another marked stile opposite and go up the next field bearing over to the left. (The field may be divided up into separate horse grazing paddocks). Cross another stile and then go across to the hedge on the far side and follow it along on your left and then strike across the field to reach the right of a bungalow. Cross the stile onto the lane. Turn right and come into the village of Greet.

❼ Greet At the junction turn left in Market Lane. At the main junction in the centre of the village find the very welcoming Harvest Home opposite, open for lunch every day.

Go down Greet Road at the side of the pub. Once you have crossed the railway, take the footpath marked on the right. Go along a few yards alongside the railway and then turn left away from the line going up a field, following the right hedge. Cross a stile in the corner onto a lane. Turn right. After eight minutes, just before a turning on the right, go left through a gate close to the footpath sign. Head up the field to the top right corner. Go through the metal gate on the right, just short of the corner and reach a track.

❽ Track Turn left uphill. Go through a gate and continue on up. Pass the drive to Abbot Leys Farm and carry on – the track is more of a footpath now. Go through a gate into the edge of woodland. Turn left on a track and after a few yards, fork left again following the Wychavon Way following it down with a wall on your left

and trees on the right and then down through a field. Go through a kissing gate in the corner and continue downhill – don't bear right. There are great views over Winchcombe. Cross a stile and head down, bearing slightly right to a metal kissing gate. Turn left down the lane and come into Winchcombe. Turn left at the junction – still on the Wychavon Way. At the next junction, turn right and soon reach the main road. Go left passing the attractive stone cottages of Winchcombe, and also the Railway Museum.

Pass Winchcombe Abbey and reach the market cross and continue on, soon coming to Cowl Lane. Turn left, retracing your steps of earlier back to the car park.

Sudeley Castle and gardens are open from Easter to October
Tel: 01242 602308

The Harvest Home, Greet.
Tel: 01242 602430

Winchcombe Railway Museum.
Open weekends in the afternoon, Easter to October and at other selected times.
Tel: 01242 620641

From Long Barrow to ancient church

Belas Knap – Brockhampton – Charlton Abbots – Belas Knap

About 8.5 miles. 4 hours walking.

OS Outdoor Leisure map 45, the Cotswolds, Ref: 019 263

Skylarks sung high overhead for most of this peaceful and picturesque circle in the Cotswolds just south of Winchcombe. It's an easy Cotswold round with only a couple of steady uphill sections, neither very long or steep. The rest is flat on easy dry paths and quiet lanes with changing vistas over the hills as you go. We start with views over Sudeley Castle and climb to visit an ancient restored Long Barrow near the start and then wend out way across a Cotswold plateau splashed bright yellow with

banks of gorse to come down to the small church and manor of Sevenhampton and then on to a 17th Century inn at Brockhampton about half way round (two hours). Then, in my view, the most beautiful part of the walk unfolds. In the small hamlet of Charlton Abbots there is a chance to visit an ancient restored church as an added bonus and then we walk along the edge of a hill with softer views over the folding fields, combes and streams.

START at the parking lay-by for Belas Knap long barrow. This is signed by English Heritage and is up narrow **Corndean Lane** which leads off the Winchcombe-Cheltenham **B4632** road just south of Winchcombe. The lane is signposted to the long barrow and to Brockhampton and Andersford. You pass **Winchcombe Cricket Club ground**, follow the lane up and turn left towards Belas Knap and then see the lay-by on the left opposite the Belas Knap sign. It is not very large and you are warned not to leave valuables in the car. There is a great view here over **Winchcombe** and **Sudeley Castle**.

❶ **Belas Knap car park** Cross the road and take the marked Cotswold Way footpath opposite over a stile and up through woodland. Go through a metal hunting gate and now follow the left edge of the field along and then uphill. There are glorious views unfolding behind. Continue to hug the left edge and near the top you will find yourself on a path with a hedge of bushes and small trees on the right. On the left is woodland, full of bluebells when I came here. Go through another metal gate and over a stone stile to reach Belas Knap. Go over the stone stile on the marked Cotswold Way and follow the right wall along in the field. At the end turn left on the track. After about half a mile come down to a deserted old stone Cotswold farm, Wontley Farm.

❷ **Deserted farm** Continue ahead on the main track ignoring side turns. After

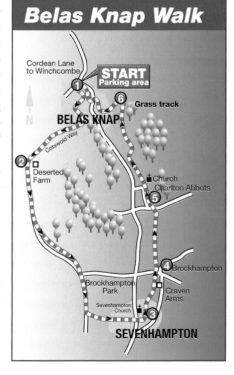

Belas Knap Walk

about two-thirds of a mile of good open walking with widespread Cotswold views you reach a small parking area and a lane at Cleeve Hill Common. Continue ahead on the lane which again offers the chance to stride out and enjoy good vistas at the same time.

Ignore the turn to Brockhampton. Continue on the lane past a farm and after about another seven minutes, turn left on the bridleway. Follow the left edge of the field along and down starting to get views over Sevenhampton and Brockhampton. Over on your left in the next field but one was the site of the medieval village of Sennington. Go through a metal gate and continue on

down the left hedge. Go through another gate and on in the same direction with the wall on your right. Pick up a path which leads down to the road. Cross and go ahead towards the church.

❸ Sevenhampton Church Pass the Manor House and go left into the church yard on the footpath to Brockhampton which goes to the right side of the church. St Andrew's church is interesting with a board listing the incumbents right back to 1204 It dates back to the 12th Century, with much rebuilding in the 15th Century when the perpendicular tower and transepts were added. The three bells are

of particular note still hanging in their original wooden frames. One of them, dedicated to St Gabriel, has been ringing out in Sevenhampton since the early 15th Century.

Take the footpath past the church and go out of a kissing gate and on along the left wall, through another kissing gate and continue on along the wall in pleasant park-like country. Go through another kissing gate and continue to head down this field, bearing over to the right edge by a stream. Follow the right edge along and in the corner go out right through a metal kissing gate and up a footpath to reach a tarmac drive and then the Craven Arms in Brockhampton.

❹ **Brockhampton** This 17th Century hostelry serves good food at lunchtime and in the evenings. Continue past the pub and reach a junction with the main village road. Turn right and then almost immediately left by the small triangle of green with a phone box and smart millennium stone post box plinth. Along here is the village hall.

Carry on to the corner and go straight ahead through a metal kissing gate.

Follow the well marked path straight ahead for well over half a mile through fields. En route, at the first white tipped footpath sign stay in the field with hedge on left. At the second marker go into the field at the side and continue in the same direction, this time with the hedge on your right. Come out onto a lane, turn left immediately turn right to Charlton Abbots.

⑤ Charlton Abbots At the bend of the road in this hamlet go straight ahead up the no through road. It's worth making a small detour right down the footpath to the pretty 13th Century church tucked away down below and which was open when I came here. It had fallen into disrepair and disuse by the 18th Century but had a number of restorations and is now a beautiful and peaceful tiny country church.

To continue the walk, carry on along the no through road and at the end take the marked footpath through the gate to the left of the cottage. Follow this track along climbing gently. Go through a gate and continue on along the fence line. Cross a stile and go to the right of a cottage.

Come onto a grassy track and turn right

© Clint Hughes

6 Grassy track Turn sharp left up this steadily uphill track, through another gate and on and up to the top.

Turn right through a gate and follow this track, with woodland on the left, still climbing gently for a very short while. Pass in front of a cottage which enjoys panoramic views across towards Winchcombe and Sudeley Castle. At the end of the cottage turn up left on another track which brings you up to the lane at the top. Turn right on the lane and after about a third of a mile reach the parking area where you began.

The Craven Arms, Brockhampton, Tel: 01242 820410

along here. Come up left to another track with a footpath arrow and go across to a hunting gate. Cross the field and go over a stile on the other side. Follow the arrow down the centre of the field and on the far side cross a stile. Continue straight ahead across fields. Drop down into a band of woodland by a stream where you cross two stiles. After the second stile, bear up right to the very top right corner and over another stile, again marked with an arrow. The path goes up into the field then heads straight across to a line of ash and oak which once presumably formed a continuous boundary. Follow the line of trees and when they end, continue on in the same direction across the field. As you drop down towards a cottage, before leaving the field, reach a crossing grassy track.

Circling through the Slaughters

Burton-on-the-Water – Upper Slaughter – Lower Slaughter
– Burton-on-the-Water

About 2.5 miles. 2.25 hours walking.

OS Outdoor Leisure Map 45, the Cotswolds, Ref 167 206

Upper and Lower Slaughter with their thatched cottages are quintessential Cotswold villages by a clear river. They certainly are idyllic but this beauty has meant an influx of visitors and they are best visited out of season or in the week so you can explore in slightly more peaceful surroundings. This easy walk circles round from Burton-on-the-Water and brings us on foot into the Slaughters without adding yet another car to the already congested parking in the two tiny villages. We follow the Windrush Way out of Burton and then cross over into the valley of the River Eye where Upper and Lower Slaughter or an old Mill which serves simple lunches and also plenty of places back in Burton. It's not an away-from-it-all walk, but is certainly very pleasing on the eye walking by the clear Windrush, and easy underfoot too. This is a good walk for the morning or afternoon.

You may need to park in one of the major pay car parks, which unfortunately aren't cheap, but roadside parking will only allow you two hours, not quite enough. Make your way to the High Street where the River Windrush flows so picturesquely.

① High Street Walk south down the High Street with the river on your left and cross over the river on a bridge at the Motor Museum. On your left are the old Manse and the Duke of Wellington on your right. Continue along this street and shortly turn right on the Windrush Way public footpath. Come to the river and follow it along on your right. Keep on following signs, crossing back over the river and follow it along on your right. Keep on following the signs, crossing back over the Windrush and coming eventually to a residential road. Turn left on this with the river over on your left.

Reach the main road, the A429 and follow the footpath opposite – still the Windrush Way. Keep on for about half a mile. Come to a gate and follow the footpath, still the Windrush Way, up to the right. Go through woodland and meet a junction of paths. Here leave the Windrush

Way and take the Gloucestershire Way and bridleway up to the right through the trees, climbing gently through the valley.

② **Road** Follow this through fields for over half a mile until you arrive at a road. Cross and turn left for a few minutes. Take the first turn right towards Upper and Lower Slaughter, heading down towards Upper Slaughter – you can just see the village church tower soaring out of the valley of the River Eye below.

Then down at the end of the lane you spy a glorious gabled Manor House which is one of the finest buildings in the area. The oldest part of the house dates from the 15th Century but the front is Elizabethan. The Manor is now a hotel. However, we are not going that way! Half way down the hill, turn left on a track which goes gently uphill. Go through a gate across the track and immediately turn right, through a metal gate marked with a footpath arrow and head down the field along the left fence all the way to the edge of the village. Come out of the field at a junction and go straight down to the village.

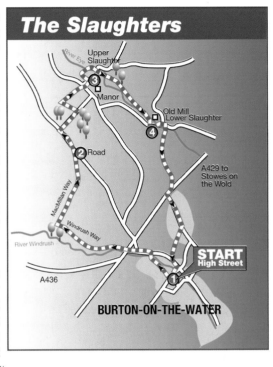

The Slaughters

③ **Upper Slaughter** Turn left into the small village square surrounded by cottages designed by Sir Edward Lutyens in 1906, and go up the path to the peaceful little church which dates back to the 12th Century, but there have been a number of partial rebuilds and renovations. There are three brasses to the Slaughter family, and a small shield with the Slaughter arms dated 1698 up by the altar. The name Slaughter comes from the old English word for a wetland or "slough".

The village has typical Cotswold stone houses with dormers, mullions and dripstones and just to the east of the church, excavations have revealed that there was once a Norman Castle.

Come out of the church and follow the path with the church on your left and go through a gate and down the lane in the village. Turn left and drop down to the River Eye which you cross at the side of the ford. Go right over a stile and along a path through rough ground by the

© Clint Hughes

river, full of wild flowers in the spring and summer. Cross another stile and reach a lane. Turn right over the river and after about a minute uphill turn left on the marked Warden's Way. Cross over the Eye once more and go through a gate into a field and forking right on the Warden's Way. Follow this through fields with the water over on your right. Come closer to

© Clint Hughes

the river just before you come into Lower Slaughter.

④ Lower Slaughter Reach the Old Mill museum, gift and craft shop and café which serves light lunches and teas in an idyllic riverside position.

A jazz singer, Gerald Harris, runs the whole venture. Go down past the mill, noting the old millwheel, and pick up the slab walkway next to the river that brings you to a very pretty part of the village. Pass the old village pump on your left. Cross a road and continue along with the river to your right. Cross the river and follow the public bridleway and Warden's Way towards Burton-on-the-Water. Go through a gate and follow the Warden's Way, which continues to be a tarmac path across fields to the main road. Turn right onto the road for a few yards and cross at the lights and go in to Station Road towards Burton, walking along the pavement for a few minutes. Cross and take the marked Heart of England Way path down on the right. This path passes a school and also parish church and reaches the heart of the village. Turn left to finish where you started.

Old Mill Museum
Gift and craft shop and café.

© Clint Hughes

Water-Meadows

Water-Meadows car park – Great Rissington – car park

5.8 miles. 2.75 hours walking.

OS Outdoor Leisure Map 45 The Cotswolds, ref:175 153

The restored water-meadows alongside the River Windrush on the Sherborne estate run by the National Trust are an interesting start to this pretty Cotswold circle. They support a wide variety of birdlife and other interesting insects and animals. The walk goes through Great Rissington village where the attractive Old Lamb Inn makes a great stop. There is an optional bird hide to visit and wide open views and a sense of space unlike the cosier feel of the combes in other parts of the Cotswolds. There is a steady but not difficult ascent to Great Rissington and then a similar descent on the way back over the Rissington with a climb up onto the top back to the National Trust car park.

START at the National Trust Water-Meadows car park just to the north of Sherborne village which lies off the A40 road between Northleach and Burford. Go to the village of Sherborne, pass the small Post Office on your left and take the first turn left signed to Clapton on the Hill. About half a mile up here is Northfield Barns and the car park just past this on the left.

❶ National Trust car park

Turn right from the car park back the way you came up from Sherborne and just past the farm turn left on a public bridleway. There's a real feel of parkland here with beautiful trees. Drop steadily down-hill for just under 0.75 miles to a National Trust information board about the Water-Meadows.

❷ Water-Meadows These

lie here alongside the River Windrush and were a system of sluices, carriers and drains to flood the riverside fields and produce large amounts of good quality grass for sheep and cattle. The system as a whole dates back to the late 16th Century in Southern England, although the creation of meadows here at Sherborne was much later in 1844. They fell into disuse in the early 1900s due to changes in farming practices.

Eventually in 1992, the National Trust with the help of the Countryside Stewardship scheme, began to restore 149 acres of these old water-meadows. The newly sown meadow grasses support numerous insects including butterflies. The ditches are valuable wetland habitat for dragonflies, damsel flies and other creatures needing slow moving waters. In particular, the meadows are most valuable for birdlife, for

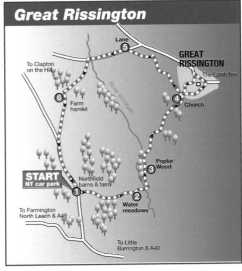

Great Rissington

© Clint Hughes

wading birds such as Redshank, Lapwing and Snipe and larger Curlew. They have also become a favourite hunting ground for barn owls looking for small mammals such as mice and voles.

(For a quick detour to see more of the water-meadows, go left alongside one of the drainage on the marked path and follow signs on another path on the right leading to the bird hide)

Continue our circle by continuing ahead crossing the water-meadows and soon cross the River Windrush. Continue on. The path bends and reaches a footpath marker post. Go into the field and immediately turn left along the edge. The Windrush

is meandering along on our left although somewhat obscured by vegetation at this point. It is very tranquil walking with not a building in sight. Continue on until you cross a little bridge, go through a gate and enter a poplar wood.

❸ **Poplar Wood** Follow the path through the edge of the poplars with the river still on your left. It would be a good spot for a picnic. Reach a marked footpath on the right out of the wood. Go up the right edge of the field starting the uphill leg of the walk to Great Rissington. At an oak tree, bear across the field and on the far side turn right up the edge for a short way. Follow the footpath arrow into the next field across the centre,

still climbing steadily. Aim for woodland on the top. You are very close to Great Rissington although it is hidden from view. At the top, reach a drive with leylandii trees on either side. Turn right up the drive. As the drive bends right to a farm, go ahead following the yellow arrow through a gate. Turn left alongside beautiful country homes converted from farm buildings. Reach the church.

For a visit to the pub and to the village, go up the road uphill, ignoring the fork left, past pretty cottages to reach the green in the village and on the left the Lamb Inn. Continue past the Lamb on the

road, which bends round and then take, the first turn left. This brings you back to join the road just above the church. Go back to the church. Ahead is the glorious manor of Great Rissington.

4 Church Pass the church porch and entrance and continue on along the concrete path away from the church. Go through a small wood and on the other side follow the arrow on through another field, and then across into another small wood. Go over a footbridge onto a track. Cross and head across the field on the other side in the same direction as before. At a corner, go ahead with ditch and hedge on your right. Bend left round the first corner in the field still following the hedge. Just before the next corner, go right over the ditch on a marked footbridge. Cross a stile and follow the left edge of the field for a short distance and then go left over a marked footbridge. Cross a stile and follow the left edge of the field for a short distance and then go left over a marked footbridge and follow the arrow right down the length of the field. The stile is towards the end of the left hand side. Cross the stile and then head across the next field in more or less the same direction as before heading for the far right side somewhere near the centre. Cross a stile onto the lane.

© Clint Hughes

© Clint Hughes

6 Farm Go round the corner and just before you leave the farm collection, just opposite the Old Granary, turn left on a public footpath track. Go into the field and follow the right hedge all the way along two fields with good views back across towards Great Rissington and across the area where you have been walking. Reach a lane and turn left. Ignore a footpath on the right and just follow the lane back to the car park.

The Lamb Inn, Great Rissington
Tel: 01451 820388

5 Lane Turn left on this little used lane. Cross over the Windrush over a stone bridge and immediately turn left on the public footpath. Go along a short length of path and then cross over a stile. Go diagonally up across the field and over another stile. Go over a wide belt of grass and follow the arrow uphill. Cross a stile to the left of a corner sticking out into the field. And then head up across the next field in the same direction as before heading to just below the top left corner near to a farm. Cross onto a drive and turn up right towards a "hamlet" of converted homes at Broadmoor Farm.

From the Roman villa

Chedworth Roman Villa – Withington – Roman Villa

6 miles. 3 hours walking.

OS Outdoor Leisure Map 45 The Cotswolds, ref: 054 136

This easy circle sets off from Chedworth Roman Villa and climbs gently through trees to the open top and then heads across an old bomber airfield before dropping down to the picturesque honey–coloured village of Withington set by the River Colne. Here the Mill Inn has been serving travellers for more

than 400 years. It has a peaceful setting alongside the millstream with cosy, flagstone and beamed bars and open fires inside and a wonderful garden for warmer weather. On the return, we follow a quiet lane and then a pretty footpath through fields before following the old railway line back to the Villa. There is only some gentle climbing and the going is good underfoot. Allow time to visit the Villa which is open from March to November every day except Mondays.

1 Villa From the forest car park go down steps and then turn left on the drive to the Roman Villa. Pass the Villa on your right and take the footpath at the side which climbs uphill through trees. Go under the tunnel under the old railway line. (You return this way from the old line down the steps) Reach a junction of paths and keep straight on, still climbing up through the woodland. Near the top, still just in the woods, meet a crossing grassy track. Turn left and then immediately right following a yellow footpath arrow. Continue uphill into a field.

2 Old airfield As you keep straight you see evidence of the former bomber airfield with remains of some of the airstrips. In fact, you pick up one of these tarmacadamed strips and continue straight on following the left fence. Ignore a stile on the left. Bend right, still on the tarmac and still following the left fence of the old airfield. Ignore an arrow going left. Just continue on the tarmac. Before the track bends left, reach footpath marker posts. Turn right following the yellow arrow across the open top of the airfield. It is good high open walking, a good contrast to the earlier climb up through woods. Reach more footpath arrows. Keep straight ahead (not diagonally right) roughly in the same direction as before. Go through a squeeze stile onto a small lane.

3 Lane Cross the lane and go over the stile opposite, following the concrete drive ahead. At the metal gate across the drive, don't go through, but instead turn right on the marked path between barbed wire and a hedge. Turn left in woodland and follow the path out into a field. Turn right along the right edge of the field with woodland at the side. Cross a stile by a gate and go over the

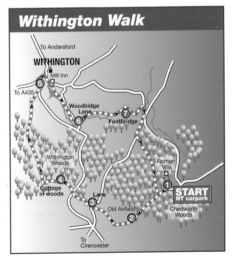

Withington Walk

lane and up the drive to Woodlands Farm marked as a bridleway. Take the path through a gate ahead on the right and follow a grassy bridleway passing a satellite mast on your left. Continue walking along in the edge of woodland.

4 **Cottage in woods** Pass a pretty cottage and continue on. After a few more minutes come into an open grassy area. Ignore the grassy track immediately on the right and go on a few more yards and turn right on the marked footpath. Follow this through woodland until you come to a junction with broad crossing track. Turn right (there was no marking at this point when I came here). Pass pheasant pens and start to descend. Leave woodland through a gate and immediately turn left on the marked path.

Go ahead through the field bearing away from the top edge and heading for a large pylon in the field. Ahead down in the valley you can see some of the rooftops of Withington and the church tower. Go through into the next field, passing just to the right of the pylon and head diagonally right down to a good solid wooden kissing gate. Once through, head across the field to the far left corner and cross a stile onto a lane on the edge of the village. You are about 1hr 30 minutes walking time from the start.

© Clint Hughes

5 **Withington** Turn left. Follow the lane, ignoring the first turn right, and bend round to the right going past some of the pretty cottages in Withington. The settlement grew up along the River Colne and from about the 13th Century sheep farming and the wool industry were the villager's main source of income, along with forestry. It was a community largely cut off from the outside world with occasional visiting carters, farmers and peddlers. Life began to change in the late 19th Century when a regular carrier service was started to Cheltenham and

Circencester and then in 1891 the village changed forever when the mixed gauge railway came through the Colne Valley. At a junction in the village reach the school on the left. The church opposite is usually open and has a fine selection of hand stitched kneelers and a book explaining the kneeler designs. Turn right down the hill on the main road soon reaching the welcoming Mill Inn beautifully situated by the River Coln. Continue past the pub and opposite the car park by a red phone box turn right up steps on the footpath. Stay on this through a kissing gate and dropping down to come alongside a large pond. The path continues along with the pond down on the right and takes you over a stile and into the garden of Riverside Cottage. Go out up to the lane and turn right. There is now a pretty walk for a few minutes along this quiet lane, paralleling the old railway line up on the left.

⑥ Woodbridge Lane Come to Woodbridge Lane on the left and go under the brick railway bridge. Continue on until just before a house turn left over a stile on the marked path. Follow this well signed path through woodland and through fields.

⑦ River Footbridge Reach the River Colne and cross on a footbridge. Go over a stile and follow the path left along the fence with the river on your left. In the corner opposite beautiful Cassey Compton house cross a stile (or go through a gate further to the right) onto the lane. Turn right and shortly turn right on the lane to Chedworth and Cirencester and climb uphill. At the top carry on and just before a railway bridge, go left on a small unmarked path into woodland. It winds through and comes down to the old railway line which is now a nature reserve. Turn left and follow the old line until you reach a big information board about the Reserve. Turn left down the steps. Turn right on the path back down to the Roman Village.

The Mill Inn, Withington
Tel 01242 890204

© Clint Hughes

Beautiful Bibury

Bibury (Arlington) – Coln St Aldwyns – Bibury

6.3 miles. about 3.30 hours walking.

OS Outdoor Leisure Map 45, the Cotswolds, ref: 117 066

The wide open spaces of the Oxfordshire Cotswolds and the clear waters of the Colne river await us on this circle of good, easy walking on dry tracks with changing scenery and historic beauty. We circle round from Bibury, described by William Morris as the most beautiful village in England, and walk on dry tracks with good open views to the beautiful village of Coln St Aldwyns. Here there is an outstanding old coaching inn and fine food, pretty cottages and an interesting church. Then it's back through the valley following the clear Coln River before reaching old Bibury at magnificent Bibury Court, and the church. You will feel you have had a good walk and enjoyed much beauty, but there are no real uphills or difficult terrain. At the start you visit medieval weavers cottages and at the end you could look round a 17th Century mill and a trout farm. It's a good doggy circle, too.

START at the Arlington end of Bibury which lies on the B4425 Cirencester to Burford road. Park along the road by the River Colne near the footbridge across to Arlington Row. If there is no space, you may be able to park by the trout farm or mill. If you park by the mill take the footpath along the River Colne, keeping it on your left until you come to Arlington Row and turn right up the lane. If parking along the road by the river, cross the pretty stone bridge over the Coln and carry on to the Row.

❶ **Arlington Row** There's a good information board about Arlington Row and Rack Isle, this low lying meadow, called after the wooden racks that were used to stretch the drying cloth at Arlington Mill. Arlington Row, a row of medieval weavers' cottages, is cared for by the National Trust and are perhaps the most photographed cottages in the country. Ignore side footpaths and continue ahead uphill up the small lane away from Arlington Row, passing more pretty cottages. At a small triangle of grass turn left on a drive which is marked as a public footpath to Ready Token. Go through a metal gate and ahead on the

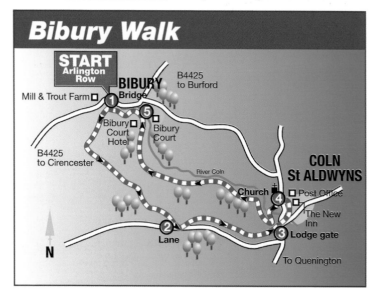

Bibury Walk

START
Arlington Row

BIBURY
Bridge

B4425
to Burford

Mill & Trout Farm ❶

Bibury Court Hotel

❺

Bibury Court

B4425
to Cirencester

River Coln

COLN St ALDWYNS

Church ❹ ☐ Post Office

The New Inn

❷
Lane

❸ Lodge gate

To Quenington

N

© Clint Hughes

path. Follow the right hedge and at the end of the field keep straight on, still with hedge on right. The views are pleasant and open and the air is exhilarating.

This field is a big one and at the end, turn left on a track following the wall and hedge on your right. Keep on in this direction along the edge of fields on a good, dry track. After just over half a mile it starts to drop downhill. Cross a stile by a gate and follow the grassy track gently uphill, through another gate and onto a lane.

❷ **Lane** Turn left for a couple of minutes and just past cottages and a lodge go left through a gate on a bridleway. Go to the right down the length of the field, crossing to the far corner near which is a large metal gate marked with a blue arrow (don't by mistake take the yellow arrowed stile out of the field). You are aiming to the left of the farm. Go through the gate on a grassy track past the farm buildings and a cottage on your left and

cross straight over the drive. Keep ahead and go straight across two fields. Go through a gate and then follow the right wall through park-like countryside with a beautiful tract of woodland down on the left. Go through a gate and follow the track downhill to the River Coln*. (If you want to shorten the walk and leave out Coln St Aldwyns, go straight to the next asterisk). To go up into Coln St Aldwyns, the pub and church, leave by a gate by the lodge.

❸ **Lodge Gate** Go through to road. Turn left, cross the river and follow the pavement up into the pretty village, passing the old and very popular New Inn. Keep on up to the post office and a chestnut tree on an island of grass in the middle of the road.

Turn left by the post office and then shortly left on the lane to the church. There is a wonderful line of stone cottages built in memory of Lucy Catherine,

© Clint Hughes

Countess of Aldyn. If you wan to visit the church, opposite these cottages, go right and under a stone arch.

❹ **Church** This church has an unusual dedication as the church of the decollation (beheading) of St John the Baptist. Inside the font is of interest, with a Greek palindrome round the foot (which means it reads both ways).

Return to the lane by the memorial cottages and turn right. Or if you didn't visit the church, just keep straight on. The lane runs into a public footpath which goes downhill and across the River Colne

to a track. Turn left and come back to the road where you were earlier. Retrace your earlier steps by going right over the bridge and right by the lodge. Now just follow the river walking through a long field with woodland left and the river right. It's a very beautiful and peaceful spot.

Go ahead into woodland through a five bar wooden gate and follow the path through the woods and on out the other side. Keep on with the woodland left along a big field and in the next field start to come closer to the river again. Keep following the river. Go through a gate, ignoring a private footbridge over the river. For a while the river bears away somewhat. Go through a gate and hug the edge of the wood and go through another gate and straight across the field towards another wood.

Cross a footbridge and slab stile and now just follow the path up through woods and on for about half a mile. Reach a big gate with a yellow footpath arrow. Go through and downhill with a glorious view ahead of a fine Cotswold mansion, Court Farm. Ignore side tracks.

After going through another gate, the track becomes made-up. Pass a lodge house and the entrance to Court Farm

© Clint Hughes

and down to the picturesque mill. Cross the river on a bridge by a weir and enjoy a stunning view of Bibury Court.

⑤ Bibury Court This gracious Tudor mansion is now a hotel (since 1968). Sir Thomas Sackville built the main part

© Clint Hughes

in 1633; the interior was remodelled in 1759 and again after 1922 Sir Thomas, an illegitimate son of the 1st Earl of Dorset, was "a Knight and a gentleman-usher to James 1", Charles II is reputed to have visited the court when he attended Bibury Races, as did the Prince Regent during the reign of George III.

The house remained in the Sackville family for several generations and through the female line passed to the Cresswells, who eventually, owing to a disputed will and years of litigation, sold the house in the last century to Lord Sherbourne. Charles Dickens is said to have written 'Bleak House' with the court case in mind. After various owners, and the death of Lady Clark – the last person to use it as a private house – the court was turned into a luxury hotel in 1968.

© Clint Hughes

Carry on along the drive, climbing gently to a t-junction. Turn left and come to the main road. Turn left and shortly at the beginning of the hotel drive go right by a phone box and alongside the green by more pretty cottages and carry on to the church. You can see more of Bibury Court as you walk through the churchyard to the main church entrance behind.

The church of St Mary's is a fine building dating back to Saxon times, the interior of which fortunately escaped restoration

by the Victorians. There is much of architectural and historic interest including the eye-catching timbered roof.

Come out of the church gate and turn left, continuing the route you were on and follow the lane out to the main road. Turn back to where you started.

The New Inn, Coln St Aldwyns
Tel: 01285 750651

Have a cheese roll on the cheese roll slope!

Birdlip Picnic Site − Cooper's Hill − Cranham − Birdlip − picnic site
About 10.5 miles. About 5.25 hours walking.

OS Explorer Map 179, Gloucester, Cheltenham and Stroud, ref: 931 154

A magnificent, leafy, all-day walk along good tracks on the edge of the Cotswolds, east of Gloucester and south of Cheltenham, with great views from the escarpment and a lot of walking in beautiful beech and other woodland. You climb up to reach the top of the famous Cheese Roll slope- a good picnic spot − but that is the only really steep ascent. And is quite short. The rest is the usual Cotswold mix of up and down, following the Cotswold Way and also a local Walking for Pleasure woodland route, which has a magic at any time of year. Autumn has the glory of tree colour and fungi; winter has the advantage of airy woods, the beautiful shapes of bare trees and good views; Spring brings bluebells, wild garlic and wood anemones and in Summer the woods and countryside are clad in glorious shades of green. There is a fine pub en route in Cranham village and we also visit Birdlip.

START at the Birdlip Picnic Site, also known as **Barrow Wake** free car park, just north of **Birdlip village, just off the A417**, about half a mile to the south of the very busy Air Balloon park at the junction of the **A417 and A436**. It's signed as a side road to Birdlip and may not have any signs saying **Barrow Wake**. It is a long stay parking area and a magnificent viewpoint. Drive in and go under the metal barrier to find a parking bay. There are information boards about the escarpment and view. Remember, don't leave valuables in your car.

❶ Birdlip picnic site and car park
Follow the escarpment along, keeping the valley down on your right and going through the grassy, bumpy area of Barrow Wake enjoying widespread vistas. Cross a stile, go through a field and then another stile brings you into woods. You are following the yellow arrow and white blob of the Cotswold Way. Stay in woodland and soon at a wooden footpath signpost, take a short extra leg out to the Peak, which is a grassy knoll high on the edge (but requires no further climbing!) and from there you have an unrivalled panorama to take your breath away (literally − if it's windy!). Return to the wooden sign and continue on the Cotswold Way through woodland.

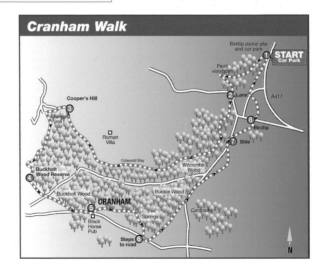

Cranham Walk

❷ Lane Come down to cross a lane and take the Cotswold Way opposite, dropping downhill. Meet a t-junction of tracks and turn left. It's a three mile stretch now on the Cotswold Way to the hamlet of Cooper's Hill, on woodland tracks and at one point, along a vehicle track. There are some pleasant views through the trees from time to time and the woodland is mixed and pretty. At one stage you cross right to Witcombe reservoir and nearby, just below a farmhouse, see remains of Great Witcombe Roman Villa in a field by a farmhouse. It dates from the 3rd Century AD and was the centre of a nobleman's country estate not far from the city of Glevum, modern day Gloucester. Extensively modernised in the late 4th Century AD, the complex was finally abandoned in the 5th Century AD.

The mosaics can be seen on certain days of the year.

❸ Cooper's Hill Come to the edge of the hamlet and pass the friendly Rose's tea garden which is usually open – you might need a drink for the climb ahead! Reach a postbox left, and then fork left onto Cooper's Hill Common following the sign to Painswick. Pass behind a cottage and go through a hunting gate into the nature reserve. Climb steeply on the Cotswold Way through woodland to the top of the Cheese Roll Slope where a cockerel crowns the pole there. Each Spring Bank Holiday, Double Gloucester cheeses in round cases are rolled down the hill pursued by enthusiastic runners. There's a good view across the vale with Gloucester round to the left.

Follow the yellow/orange arrow away from the edge. The orange stripe on the arrow indicates that it is a local woodland walk, but it is also still the Cotswold Way. After about another mile of woodland walking, you hear the sounds of traffic on a nearby road. Keep following the yellow/orange arrow.

❹ **Buckholt Wood Reserve** Reach the sign for the Reserve. Shortly past this, there is a fork of tracks. We leave the Cotswold Way and fork left still following the yellow and orange arrow. Drop downhill and cross a road. Follow the arrowed path left through woods to reach a road on the edge of Cranham village. Turn left along the road into the village.

❺ **Cranham** The name Cranham is derived from the Old English for 'homestead of the crane or heron. Each year on the second Monday in August the village holds its Cranham feast and Deer Roast. It is also the site of Gloucestershire's county scout campsite. Soon you come to a small lane going up right to the welcoming Black Horse pub. It serves food at lunchtimes daily – an ideal resting and recovery spot. At the pub, turn left and the tiny lane takes you back to the main village road you were on before, turn right. (Or to miss out the pub, simply stay on the road you were on). Continue on to reach the common at the telephonebox, by the village pond. Turn left along the bottom of Cranham Common. After the last cottage, follow our arrow

© Clint Hughes

along the right fork, keeping the woods on your left. On the far side of the common, the path takes you onto a well-used track through more glorious woodland with a valley down on the left. After a while the path changes in nature and becomes quite narrow, and lined with sedges and grasses walking in an open area between flanks of woodland. It can be boggy in parts near Many Well springs, which is the source of the Painswick Stream.

⑥ Steps to road Follow the path for about a mile, going up steps at the end to a road. Turn left for just over 100m and then turn left by a house following the track marked by the orange tailed arrow. Follow this path with fields on the right and continue on staying just inside woodland. Eventually you pass on the right a small camp site. Keep on through a narrow grassy strip. Keep to the right and follow the arrow out to the road. Turn left along the road for about 300 yards. Bear right down onto a small path which continues on through woodland paralleling the road and with fields on the right. It gradually bears further from the road. Just past a field gate on the right, follow the marked path left. Pass cottages over on the right and go through an open area and then join a track leading back to the road. Turn right.

⑦ Stile After a few yards, leave the yellow/orange arrow and take the first marked footpath on the right over a stile. Go ahead on the track to a barn and turn left round the far side. Shortly, climb right over a stile and head across the field to the clearly visible stile in the top corner. Continue across the next field, past the trig point, and continue on to leave the field by a stile on the far side. This route gives you a good view down over Birdlip village. Turn left on the lane, soon passing St Mary's church, which has a beautiful,

quiet simplicity inside and after a few yards reach a bend in the lane.

⑧ Birdlip Turn right down the no through road towards the school. Turn left with Birdlip Primary School on your right. Go left on the track into the cricket club ground. Turn right with the fence on your right. Cross a stile into a field and go left to reach a busy road. Cross over and follow the pavement towards the parking area, which is a long slip road and will eventually lead to where you began.

Black Horse Pub, Cranham
Tel: 01452 812217
Serves food at lunchtimes.

Cotswold contrasts

Brimpsfield – Caudle Green – Brimpsfield
5.3 miles. About 2.75 hours walking.
(If you omit the inn, the walk is a third of a mile shorter)
OS Explorer 179, Gloucester, Cheltenham and Stroud ref: 939 126

This quiet and off the beaten track walk takes us deep into Cotswold country with the contrasts of wooded valleys, bubbling streams, open high land, fields and a pretty hamlet en route. There is the option, only an extra third of a mile in total, to an old and well cared for pub which serves excellent food – about 1.75 hours from the start. At the end there is a five minute walk to a church tucked away from Brimpsfield along a footpath. Walking is undulating with only a couple of steeper sections.

© Clint Hughes

in the small village of **Brimpsfield which lies south east of Gloucester, north east of Stroud. It can easily be reached from the A417 Gloucester to Swindon road. Go to the centre of the village near a phone box and memorial cross and turn onto the road marked to Birdlip and Cheltenham. It very shortly bends and the village hall is up on the right – a small hall with a big car park.**

❶ Village Hall From here, return to the junction and the memorial cross and turn right on the Caudle Green lane. Walk through the village and ignore the turning right. Continue on the single track road straight on.

❷ Bend On the bend take the marked footpath ahead into a field. Follow the right hedge. Drop down to a metal gate with a stile at the side. Keep on, staying on the grassy track in the middle and not dropping down on the right. Soon you are walking with woodland on your right ascending into the valley. Cross a stile and follow the track with woodland on either side through this very secluded and tranquil combe. Go through a metal gate and continue through the valley. Go through another gate and now drop down right (ignoring arrow straight on)

and cross a stream and a marked stile and then follow the track left up the hill, climbing quite steeply up through the woods. The track winds its way uphill all the way to the green of the picturesque hamlet of Caudle Green.

❸ Caudle Green Go straight ahead across the green and reach the main tarmac lane. Turn right, still climbing. Look for a hunting gate on the left and a bridleway. Take this and follow the right wall, walking alongside the lane you were on for a short way. Continue to follow the right wall and at the end of the field, follow the wall round to the left and come down into a small valley. Turn right following the bridleway through the woods. Later there is a choice of tracks – take the left hand one which stays in the woods and drops down.

❹ Pond Reach a pond and carry on keeping it on your left. Continue following the stream on your left through very beautiful woodland which should be gloriously carpeted with bluebells in Spring. Eventually you reach a point where a grassy track goes off right and your track bends sharply left. Follow this track into the woods. Just before you reach the stream, turn right along a not very distinct path still with the stream on your left. It may be a little muddy in

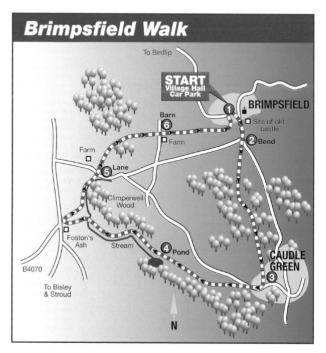

Brimpsfield Walk

To Birdlip

START
Village Hall
Car Park

① ■ **BRIMPSFIELD**

□ Site of old castle

Barn

⑥

□ Farm

② Bend

Farm □

⑤ Lane

Climperwell Wood

Farm □

Foston's Ash

Stream

④ Pond

B4070

CAUDLE GREEN

③

To Bisley & Stroud

N

parts. Carry on to a metal gate on the left (bridleway sign on right) and go through the gate.

Continue to a footbridge over the stream left. This is the way to go to visit the pub. Or you can save a total of about a third of a mile and miss the pub by just continuing straight along the track you are on for just over a third of a mile until you pass a pond on your left and then reach a lane and continue from point 5 on the Lane.

For the pub, cross the footbridge and take the path (a little over to your right) which climbs steeply up through the woods and into a field. Here there was no footpath sign when I came here but the right of way heads straight across the field bearing right and climbing up to the top edge. Go through an opening in the hedge (there may be a gate) and follow the left hedge soon reaching the garden and car park of Foston's Ash Inn.

Retrace your steps to the field and turn left around the edge to the bottom left corner. Enter the woods and follow the track which soon descends. Reach a pond on the left. Turn left, joining the track you were on earlier. Soon come to a lane.

⑤ Lane Cross and take the marked bridleway straight ahead (slightly left) through a gate into a field, keeping the farm on your left and woodland on the right. Follow the track, and just before the gate, turn up right and cross a stile marked with a yellow footpath arrow. Go through a small area of woodland and then along the edge of a field with woods on the left. Carry on in the same direction through woodland. Come into a field and follow the left hedge, climbing more gently to a stile in the left hand corner. Cross the stile and walk ahead through the next field keeping a plantation of saplings and a cricket pitch on your right. Continue on and go through a gate onto a lane with a barn and farm opposite.

⑥ Barn Cross over the lane, past the farm and barn and follow the marked bridleway. Continue ahead towards Brimpsfield to a hunting gate at the end of the field. Go through the gate and through one more fields, through another hunting gate and follow the path into the village. Turn left and come back to the

memorial cross. Over on the right is the sign to the church, a beautiful Norman church well worth a short detour.

Foston's Ash Inn
Tel: 01452 863262
Open for lunches every day.

Haresfield Hill

Shortwood topograph – Haresfield Hill – Edge – Shortwood
6.3 miles. 3 hours walking.

OS Explorer map 179 Gloucester, Cheltenham and Stroud Ref: 831 084

Magnificent Cotswold vistas along the dramatic
Southern edge of the Cotswolds with the contrast of
beech woods, bluebells, open common ground and a
pub which also enjoys great views. We start high and
stay reasonably high and there are two uphill stretches
including a fairly steep
challenge during the second
half. There are only a couple
of stiles. Be prepared for winds
as you soak up the views from
Haresfield Hill. Tracks are good
underfoot and much of the
going is on the Cotswold Way.
It's great for walking with your
dog too.

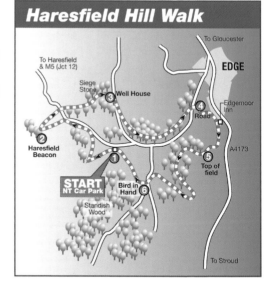

in the National Trust car park **Cripple Gate at Shortwood** – very popular with walkers. It is easy to reach the start from the M5, Junction 12 Leave the motorway and head towards Stonehouse. After a few yards only turn left down a small road. At a t-junction turn right towards Haresfield and at the village turn right again towards Haresfield Village only. Turn left up a narrow 'light vehicles only' lane leading to Haresfield Beacon. Once up the hill, go along the top for about half a mile ignoring parking lay-bys and reach a walled car park on the right.

❶ National Trust car park Go through onto the open land and head out to the topograph to enjoy sensational views. Then head away from the hill edge again, going down the other side of a 'V', imagining the topograph at the apex. Shortly before the road turn left on the marked Cotswold Way and follow this track gently downhill. Then it bears up right and after a few steps goes through a gate by the road. Turn left still on the Cotswold Way and follow it all the way out to Haresfield Beacon and a trig point at 217 metres.

❷ Haresfield Beacon This is a former Romano–British hillfort, strategically placed for defence. As you did at the topograph, imagine a 'V' shape and head back along the other arm, staying up high and heading away from the escarpment. Pick up a track along the edge of the hill and then drop down and arrive at a farm. Go out through a small yard onto the road and turn left. After a few yards, go right into the woods on the Cotswold Way. Enjoy this woodland contrast and follow the track, eventually passing the Siege of Gloucester Stone on the left.

The Siege on September 5, 1645 was one of a few during the Civil War conducted by the Royalists. Gloucester was an important strong point for Parliament, and at the time was commanded by Colonel Edward Massey, aged only 23 years, and of uncertain loyalty to Parliament, having only left Royal service in 1642. Eventually, the King abandoned the siege, and his

army marched away into the Cotswold hills having lost about 1,000 men out of a force of 35,000. It is thought the defenders lost only about 50 men, out of a total of 1,500. The cannon had little effect on the walls of Gloucester.

After about three quarters of a mile, reach the road and just before this, an 1870 well house.

❸ Well House Note the verse inside the house. Turn right on the road which climbs gently. After just under a quarter of a mile, fork left on the well marked Cotswold Way now with a blue bridleway marker. Drop down through woods with views left across the Gloucester Vale through the trees. You

follow this for about three quarters of a mile, going through Stock End Wood (National Trust) and then passing beautiful country homes on the edge of the hill. The track by this stage has become more of a drive serving the houses. Turn right on the yellow marked Cotswold Way which bends up fairly steeply and then goes on across to a road.

❹ Road Cross straight over. The Cotswold Way goes up and down the humps and bumps of former quarrying. This is high open limestone grassland with silver birches – again a real contrast to the former landscape we have been through and with great views across the valley to Painswick. Follow the Cotswold Way over two main crossing tracks dropping down the hill,

and alongside woodland on the left, going through a few trees to the third crossing track.

OPTION 1: For the pub, do a dog leg following the Cotswold Way and continuing on down to meet the road and the Edgemoor Inn. You are about 2 hours into the walk with something under another hour to go. Turn right along the road for a yard or two (left if coming from the Inn) and then cross and go back up the hill on the path marked to Scottsquar Hill and Haresfield Beacon. Reach a crossing track – which is the one you were on before dropping down to the pub. Turn left and you are on the main walk again.

OPTION 2: Turn right at this third track and follow it along, ignoring a fork which bends up right, going more or less parallel with the main road down below. Soon reach the path coming up left from the road and pub.

TO CONTINUE: The path drops gently downhill. Pass cottages and reach a tarmac lane. Go right towards Rest Haven. Before reaching the home, go up right on a marked footpath up the side of a field with hedge on right. Go over a stile and continue on up.

⑤ Top of field Go left along the fields top edge with woodland on your right. Cross a stile at the end and go through a metal gate into the edge of the wood and carry on with a metal fence on the left. Now, just follow the track along in woods for about two-thirds of a mile. Then see Pitchcombe village down on the left and ahead on the other side of the valley, the edge of Stroud. Cross a stile by a metal gate and continue for a few yards and then turn right uphill and come into a long narrow field. Continue on up climbing all the time with woodland on each side. Keep over to the left and in the top left corner, cross a stile and go up the path between walls and come up to a farm on the road at Whiteshill.

⑥ Bird in Hand Turn left and at Bird in Hand junction, fork right towards Randwick on a small road. Ignore the stile on the right but go on a few yards more and go right into the N T Standish Wood, a typical Cotswold escarpment. The path bears left and then bends into the main wood. At a main crossing track, turn right and you have now rejoined the Cotswold Way although not marked as such at this point. Continue on all the way through the woods to reach your starting car park.

Edgemoor Inn,
Tel: 01452 813576

Tantalising Toadsmoor

Eastcombe − Toadsmoor − Eastcombe

About 3.25 miles. Approx 1.5 hours walking.

OS Explorer 179 map, Gloucester, Cheltenham & Stroud, ref: 891 044

Explore the quiet and picturesque Toadsmoor Valley tucked away in Cotswold country just to the east of Stroud. Here a stream flows between beech woods and grassy slopes while above idyllic mellow Cotswold stone cottages peep over the folds and from behind trees. It's a very short circle, ideal for a morning or afternoon. We start by a very popular and welcoming

pub so a visit here could be a great way to end the circle. Walking involves some fairly steep downhill lanes and paths, flat stretches on tracks − most of them dry − and then a well graded uphill return with only a couple of steep sections. My favourite time of year for this is Autumn when the valley is aglow with warm colour from the amazingly varied trees.

❶ Post Office Stores Take the No Through Road just to the left side of the Post Office Stores and it quickly becomes a narrow tarmac path which bends up to a lane. Turn left and follow this quiet lane along and then start to drop down into the valley below. Leave the cottages behind and get stunning views across the village and the wooded slopes of the valley.

The Toadsmoor Valley is one of many wooded combes which branch into the Cotswolds from the Stroud Valley and like the rest of the area flourished as a result of the woollen trade. The valley is fed by a spring yielding a never failing supply of pure water. The lane is quite steep in parts. Reach the foot, and cross the stream.

❷ Hawkley Cottage Just past the entrance to Hawkley Cottage, turn left onto a public footpath. Follow this path, narrow at first, and crossing a small stream where after rain, water flows down over a smooth rock. The path soon becomes wider and firmer taking you through the edge of woodland with the stream down below on the left, but mainly not visible at this point.

Keep on to the first large stone bridge crossing the stream. Ignore this and take the footpath straight ahead hugging the stream still. Come to a beautiful waterside

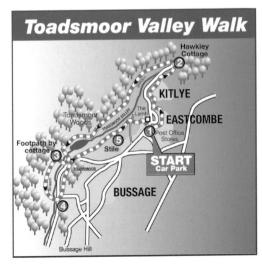

garden with Keeper's Cottage up on the right. Continue on as before and soon come to an even more beautiful spot, Toadsmoor Pond.

Keep following the main track which goes along and then left across the end of the pond and by a ford as you cross the stream. Pick up a tarmac lane/drive going uphill, passing a cottage on the right and then one on the left.

Now turn right on the first narrow tarmac lane on the right which goes back down across the stream to cottages.

❸ **Footpath by cottage** Take the narrow footpath to the left of the cottage at the end. This takes you up into woodland but before long levels out and you continue along the side of the Toadsmoor Valley as before, ignoring side paths. Descend to a t-junction of tracks, still in woodland. Turn left following the track to another large pond. Cross the stream in the area known as Toadsmoor and come up to a junction with the main road.

❹ **Bussage Hill** Cross straight over and go steeply up Bussage Hill for a few yards only (the hill leads through Toadsmoor and on up to Chalford.) Turn left along the first unmarked track which parallels the road. At the end, after two or three minutes, come out onto the road by traffic lights and cross over. Turn right a few yards and

just past the garage go left and follow the marked footpath straight ahead (ignoring the one going down left).

This well contoured track heads along the side of the hill with good views over the Toadsmoor pond and valley where you have just been, and the fields here are full of wildflowers. It then starts to ascend out of the valley, quite gently. Go through a metal gate and continue along the track and shortly, opposite a long low stone building with a corrugated iron roof, fork up right and over a stile.

5 **Stile** Climb uphill along a fenced grassy path. It soon levels out. Cross a stile onto a tarmac lane and turn steeply uphill. At a bend go left up a tarmac footpath still climbing up through the village. Turn right at the top on a lane and before long go up another tarmac footpath left through posts. Did you notice the old Red Lion pub, still with a red lion on the roof at the front, as you came up? Turn left on the lane at the top and follow this up to the green at Eastcombe, passing below the impressive village Baptist Church.

The Lamb, Eastcombe
Tel: 01452 770261

From Park to Canal

Cirencester Park – Thames and Severn Canal – Cirencester College – Park
8 Miles. 4 hours walking.

OS Explorer map 169, Cirencester & Swindon 0120313,

and OS map Explorer 168 (Stroud, Tetbury and Malmesbury).

This very varied circle starts with
a broad sweep along a wonderful
country ride in Cirencester Park
and then drops in on a saw mills
where wooden garden furniture
and gates are made. Later we
visit an interesting country pub
near a historic canal tunnel and
follow this with a walk along
the old canal, past a rural crafts
centre and through the grounds
of an agricultural college. It is easy
walking so you can stride out well
without any significant up or down hill sections and for the most part
it should be dry underfoot. It's a circle to enjoy at any time of year.
However, this is not for dogs as they are banned through some of
the park and estate.

On the southern outskirts of Cirencester at the entrance to a Caravan and Camping Club site by Cirencester Park. Approaching from the south on the A429 (Tetbury-Cirencester), at the first roundabout with A419 (Stroud-Cirencester), take the A419 left for about 50 yards, and then turn right into a wide lane (showing a Caravan Club direction sign).

❶ **Caravan site** Walk down the lane which turns to the left, passing school playing fields and then huts and the Caravan Club site. Keep on, over cattle grids and the path goes between a cricket field and tennis courts. Go through an iron kissing gate and ahead, slightly left through trees and on to a 60-yard, wide 'ride', one of many on the Bathurst Estate in Cirencester Park. Turn left and follow this very beautiful Broad Ride. Look over your shoulder and see how the tower of Cirencester Church sits squarely in the centre. This view can be seen for much of the ride. The made-up path gives way to grass. When I walked here there was a big sign banning dogs. Continue on this grassy ride for some time. Note the

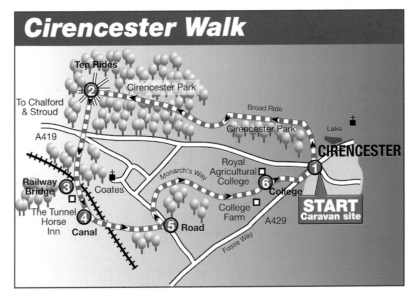

Cirencester Walk

Ten Rides

Cirencester Park

To Chalford
& Stroud

A419

Broad Ride

Cirencester Park

Lake

CIRENCESTER

Railway
Bridge ❸

Coates

Monarch's Way

Royal
Agricultural
College

❻ College

❶

Royal
Agricultural
College

The Tunnel
Horse
Inn   Canal

❹

❺ Road

College
Farm

A429

START
Caravan site

Fosse Way

various substantial shelters along this ride constructed of Cotswold stone and large enough to contain horses and their riders.

Later, on the right, there's a polo field with its small grandstand in an attractive setting. At the end of the field leave the estate track, go straight on and join the made up estate road. Turn left on the road enabling the walker or rider to navigate a short and narrow valley which ·bisects the ride. At the bottom of the hill, turn right and the track gradually swings

right through woodland until the openness of the ride is resumed.

❷ The Ten Rides

After about half-a-mile, there's a circus-like junction of the rides, known as Ten Rides. Take the wide ride which is on the left at right angles to your present path. This gradually descends towards the A419.

Cross the main road and go straight ahead, crossing a small country road, on to a track

© Clint Hughes

with a Hailey Saw Mills board. The footpath goes through the centre of the mills. There are substantial items of garden furniture and gates on display and for sale.

At the end of the last building on the left, there are two paths going ahead – don't take the larger one which veers slightly right but take the left path which goes straight into newly planted woodland and starts to descend (ignoring another left option). It is joined by another track (actually the Macmillan Way long distance path, but not signed as such at this point).

❸ Railway bridge Stay on this in the wood and before long go under a

stone bridge, which carries the London to Gloucester railway line. Bear left and continue until you come to a fairly substantial lane. On the right is the Tunnel House standing on its own at the end of the lane. The welcome is warm, the refreshments good and excellent value. Tunnellers were billeted there during the construction of the Thames and Severn Canal, in the 1700s.

❹ Canal After refreshments, with your back to the pub, take the signed track to the left of the refurbished barn, down some steps and on to the canal bank. Here is the entrance to the Sapperton Tunnel, known as the Coates Portal with a classical portico. It would not have been

a very comforting sight for those who worked on the canal as getting through it on a barge entailed lying on a plank on the barge and walking the boat along the brickwork for over two miles in the pitch dark. From 1789 when the tunnel was first used trade flourished, and despite problems with the construction and water supply, the canal and Sapperton Tunnel remained in use until the early 1900s.

This part of the canal has been restored, and if water levels permit, volunteers from the Cotswold Canal Trust run trips into the tunnel, using motorised boats and lights – a far cry from the original canal runs.

Turn right along the canal footpath to the end of the restoration. Keep on, passing

one of five original roundhouses on the canal where the linesman and their families lived. The path passes under the railway line, again under an amazing brick arch, the Skew Bridge. Continue on, soon rising to a crossing track, at an arched footbridge. The footpath to the right is the start of the long-distance Thames Walk. The river's source is about a mile down the track in the middle of a field.

However, our walk continues by crossing the bridge and immediately turning right through a gate and on to the Monarch's Way long-distance path although you won't see way-marked signs at this point. Cross three stiles with the path gently climbing with the fence on your right. You can see Trewsbury House, an attractive building, among the trees. Another stile brings you to a country road.

⑤ Road Turn left along this road and take the next road right. After about 300 yards it bends left. Immediately after this, turn right on to a sign-posted footpath, which follows a road for a few yards. As this bends to the right, the path goes ahead by the side of the Rural Crafts Centre, on to a concrete lane. The track continues on and then bends right. Follow it, passing a large milking parlour and go through usually open gates. Before long we rejoin the Monarch's Way and

© Clint Hughes

reach a farmhouse and its collection of outbuildings. The track becomes less distinct and goes ahead, bearing left down a field with a wall on your right. Go downhill past a disused quarry on the left planted with young trees.

6 **College** The track climbs gently. At a right bend go ahead and then through a squeeze stile on to a sports field, with a rugby pitch on the left. These are the grounds of the Royal Agricultural College. The path continues over the main drive, to the right of changing rooms, along a newly-made path with all-weather pitches on the right and into a mown field. Follow

the left hedge towards a Cotswold stone house. Go through the modern wooden gates to the right of the house. Turn left on to the A429 and in about 200 yards reach the roundabout, and left back to where your car was parked.

Tunnel House Inn
Tel: 01285 770280

Valley and common

Minchinhampton — Box — Amberley — Minchinhampton

About 5.25 miles. 2.7 hours walking.

OS Explorer 168, Stroud, Tetbury & Malmesbury, Ref: 007 872

Another winter winner — though good in all seasons — this circle explores several Cotswold hamlets on the slopes of the Woodchester Valley between Nailsworth and Stroud where the views across to Woodchester Park and the Nympsfield area are superb. It ends with a flat and bracing walk from Amberley across Minchinhampton Common. We use quiet lanes and tracks so there is very little chance of mud and you can stride out and give yourself a really good winter tonic. From picturesque Minchinhampton the walk drops down on lanes and through beech woods before walking along the edge of the Nailsworth valley

towards Watledge from where we climb up to the scenic area of Amberley Common and two welcoming pubs. About 45 minutes flat walk across the common, where you really get that on top of the world feeling, completes the circle. It's a dog friendly walk with no stiles, just kissing gates. There is one steep uphill section, but the rest is flat or downhill.

on Minchinhampton Common in the area known as The Park. To get there go into Minchinhampton and to the end of the High Street. Turn left past the old Crown Inn up Bell Lane with Holy Trinity church on your right and fork right to reach the common and parking area at the top.

❶ Minchinhampton Common From the parking area walk back down into the town down Bell Lane, passing the

new school on the right and the church on your left. Turn left at the junction and come to the church lychgate and a chance to visit this beautiful old church with its unusual tower. This dates from the 14th Century and there was originally a spire but it proved too heavy and so had to be partly demolished in the mid 16th Century and was finished off with a corona and pinnacles which makes it so distinctive.

Opposite the church are some convenient toilets. Reach the Market Square with the

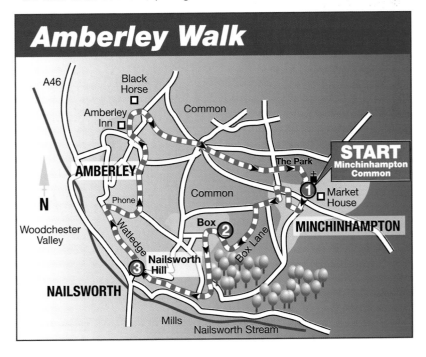

© Clint Hughes

17th Century Market House opposite, still used for a weekly market on Tuesdays. It was originally a successful wool and yarn market, but when Tetbury took the lead selling wool, Minchinhampton Fair became a sheep and cattle fair and in the 19th Century specialised in horses. As it lost its main function it became used for general town activities.

Turn right down the High Street with many fine 16th and 17th Century houses. At a junction go straight ahead down Well Hill, a reminder that here was the original supply of water for the town start to get glimpses down into the valley.

Turn right in tiny King Street, passing one of the many water outlets. This whole area is riddled with underground streams and indeed many of the houses used to have their own wells. The water tumbles down into the Woodchester Valley where many mills were established for a once prosperous woollen industry. Shortly go up right through a metal kissing gate and up the 'tunnel', a narrow walled path with three low stone arches. A kissing gate brings you to the road.

Turn left in Cuckoo Row, soon passing a coach park on the right. Take the first turning right to Box and Hampton Green. It becomes Box Lane. Before long, turn left still on Box Lane, and here you can start to enjoy good valley views.

❷ **Box** Follow the lane along into the pretty hamlet of Box down and round a right bend, and pass St Barnabas church with its distinctive gold spire. Take the first tiny lane left which descends, and shortly turn left down an even smaller tarmac path. At the end go through a kissing gate onto a footpath proper and now follow this down the hill, crossing a stone stile. Reach a lane and turn right. At the foot of Scar Hill, continue ahead on the lane. Up on your right is the edge of the extensive common.

❸ **Nailsworth** Reach a junction on the edge of Nailsworth. Cross carefully, turn right and after a few yards take the lane on the left to Watledge, and Theescombe. Follow this fairly quiet lane past honey coloured stone cottages for less than half

Image opposite © Clint Hughes

a mile, ignoring side paths. Down on your left you should be able to see the former Watledge Station.

When you reach Watledge Lodge on the left, take the marked tarmac footpath on the right by a telephone box and start the climb out of the valley. Very shortly, at a junction, turn right, still climbing. When the tarmac ends take the footpath which goes on up ahead on the left. It is quite steep so pause awhile when you reach an opening on the left which offers a good view across the valley to Woodchester.

At a lane, turn left and follow this up to a bigger lane. Turn left and then you can climb up onto the common and follow the

edge along paralleling the road down on your left.

❹ Amberley Common Reach a lane crossing the common and turn left down it to reach the first of our two Amberley pubs, the Amberley Inn, which commands a fine viewpoint. Take the cycle path at the side of the pub, paralleling the road, climbing gently. Ignore the path which drops down left.

Continue on along the side of the hill on the cycle path and then turn up right on a steep tarmac path through white topped stone posts. Reach the common and ahead on the left you can see the renowned Black Horse, a very popular

© Clint Hughes

pub with a magnificent garden with a panoramic view at the back. Turn right onto the common proper (or left if coming out of the pub) and keep over to the right by the cottages.

This common for centuries was a desolate stretch of thicket, which became a recreational area, where cricket was played, football, race meetings and even bull baiting. The earthworks of all shapes and sizes which you will see as you continue are a bit of a mystery. They may have been used by pit dwellers to protect themselves and animals, but were more likely constructed for the Romans, Saxons and Danes as Minchinhampton Common with its steep slopes would have been a good defensive position.

Turn left, passing the memorial cross on your right and reach the Amberley sign. Keep close to the stone house wall on the right. On your left is a raised area, an old British tumulus known as Whitefield's tump, where in the 18th Century the celebrated Methodist preacher, George Whitefield often preached to huge crowds.

At the corner of the house wall, walk straight across the common, continuing more-or-less the direction you were in, towards a large raised, grassed and

fenced mound which is a reservoir and which you will soon see. (You are bearing very slightly to the right). Pass the reservoir on your right and continue ahead across the common towards a road junction in the middle and a number of signposts. Do keep a wary eye out for golfers' and the direction of their swings!

⑤ Long Tom's Post When you reach the junction cross to the white post, Long Tom's Post, a well known landmark. One of the legends is that Tom Long was a highwayman, caught and hung at the scene of his crimes.

From Long Tom's Post continue ahead across the hummocky common, going

more or less in the same direction as before, with a road on each side of you. You may be able to make out a white flag pole in the distance behind a wall by houses and this is what you are heading for. Again be careful of the golfers in this area.

When you reach the flag pole and wall ahead, turn left hugging the wall on your right. Now all you do is continue to follow the wall. At one point you drop down into the ditch, and shortly after that cross a minor road. Once you have crossed this road you are in an area of the common known as the Park. Following the wall,

you will soon come back to where you parked.

The Amberley Inn
Tel: 01453 872565

The Black Horse, Amberley
Tel: 01453 872556

Image opposite © Clint Hughes

Cam challenge

Upper Cam – Cam Peak – Uley Bury fort – Uley – Upper Cam
7 miles. About 3.25 hours walking.

OS Explorer map167 Thornbury, Dursley and Yate, ref: 757 993

A challenging circle with
magnificent Cotswold scenery
taking in a peaked hill, an ancient
hill fort, enjoying great vistas and
visiting pretty Uley village with
its popular pub. After Uley, the
circle becomes more restful in
undulating countryside. The first
half of the circle involves quite a
bit of uphill work – one section
is fairly steep and the second up
to Uley Bury Fort is very steep.
However you are rewarded

with breathtaking panoramas so it is well worth doing and
should be within the capacity of most people who walk quite
regularly. In Spring there are many wildflowers to enjoy on
the grassland of the downs and fort. Try and choose a bright,
clear day so you get the views and if it is cold or windy,
wrap up well as it is exposed on the high land. Take your
time, wear good footwear and other suitable and waterproof
walking gear.

START in Upper Cam village on the edge of Dursley. Take the A4135 through Dursley, and in the Kingshill area to the west of Dursley, opposite a parade of modern shops and more or less opposite the Kingshill pub, turn left (if coming from the west from the M5, junction 14), right (if coming from the east) on the small road, Kingshill Lane, going down hill marked to Upper Cam. You may have to look quite carefully for the signpost. Follow it down and round past the Cam sign to Upper Cam and park somewhere safely near St George's church.

Cam Walk

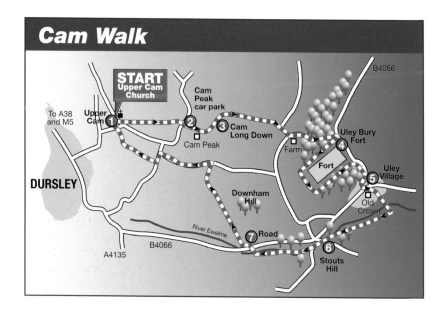

❶ Upper Cam Church From the main church entrance go left in Church Road, pass a phone box over on the right, ignore Springhill on right and turn left into Hopton Road. Immediately, take the footpath on the right up the drive of the sideways-on house, No. 45 Hopton Road. Cross the stile and follow the right hedge up the field. In the corner go through a metal kissing gate. Ignore the first stile on the right, but go ahead a yard or two and then right over a second stile and left up hill along the left hedge. When the hedge ends, continue on in the same direction up the field, heading in the direction of Peaked Down. Go through two more fields following the path and then through a wood and come onto the road.

❷ Cam Peak/Long Down car park These hills used to form part of the main Cotswold escarpment but erosion eventually caused them to be separated. Cross over into the parking area and come to the foot of Cam Peak with an interesting information board. Either go up over the peak itself where there are stunning views across to Cam Long Down, Uley Bury Fort and Downham Hill, or take the gentler climb round the left side. Reach a point where both the path from the peak and the gentler path meet and drop down into the hollow on the left where there is a signpost, and a choice of paths. Take the blue Cotswold Way sign up the sandy/stone track going uphill away from Peaked Down. It's a steady, reasonably steep climb all the way up on to Cam Long Down.

❸ Cam Long Down Once up, head along the top. It is one of the most beautiful hills I have every been on and if the weather is clear, there are glorious Cotswold views. Legend has it that beautiful Cam Long Down was the work of the devil. He took a dislike to Gloucestershire, maybe because of the number of churches, and set out to dump the Cotswolds in the Severn estuary. He started to dig up the hills and set off with his wheelbarrow full towards the River Severn, but on the way he was tired and hot and stopped to rest. A passing cobbler misled him into thinking that he still had a long journey ahead, so he decided to give up and emptied the wheelbarrow of earth on the spot – the result is Cam Long Down.

Go to the very end and follow the path left into woodland and steeply down steps. You have good views across the valley to Uley Bury Fort, your next destination!. Leave the wood over a stile under a large oak and go

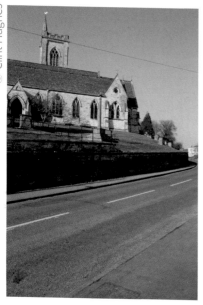

© Clint Hughes

❹ Uley Bury Fort Go right on the track up to the fort. Then bear right on the path along the long north west side of this roughly rectangular fort. Uley Bury is an Iron Age hill fort with a commanding position on the Cotswolds and was built between 2,000 and 2,500 years ago. It has a single bank and ditch enclosing a rectangular area of 32 acres and the entrance was in the northern corner where you came in. Some of the banks and ditches have been partially destroyed by quarrying.

Keep straight on with the escarpment down on your right and between the trees you will get good views back to Downham Hill, Peaked Down and Cam Long Down. Turn left and at the corner you can see, on a clear day Tyndale's monument, celebrating William Tyndale the translator of the bible.

steeply down the field towards a farm, over another stile and ahead down the edge of the next field. Cross a stile and go ahead to the road. Continue straight on along the road on the Cotswold Way. Then go left on a path toward Uley fort to Hodgecombe Farm.

At the farm buildings, follow the path straight up. It's stony and strenuous so take it slowly and just follow it all the way to the top passing a sign for the Woodland Trust. Go through to a parking area for Uley Bury Fort by the road, at this point leaving the Cotswold Way.

Along this southern edge, look out for a sunken path between two hummocks which goes down right down the side of the fort's bank. Just before the woodland, turn left on the path which runs along the side of the grassy fort with a chance to enjoy many wildflowers. It's a great spot for a picnic. Continue on the same level you were on along the side of the bank and come into woodland where the path becomes larger. Carry on until you reach a path coming down from the left and there's a yellow footpath arrow. Go right and follow the path down through the woods, immediately passing a reservoir in a wire compound on your left. Leave the woodland through a metal hunting gate and follow the path along the top of the field towards St Giles church in Uley. Follow the top edge as it kinks round and then head down across the field in the direction of the church to a wooden hunting gate in the bottom edge. Go down the path to the churchyard wall and a crossing path. Turn left and come out by the church entrance on the road.

You may care to visit this church which was rebuilt in 1857, largely with money raised by local people. It has a Norman font from an earlier church on the site.

⑤ Uley village You are about 1hr 50 minutes into the walk (walking time only!) The name Uley comes from the Anglo-Saxon for 'the open ground by the yews'. The village's prosperity was built on the woollen industry. Opposite is the village green surrounded by a number of Georgian houses and with the welcoming Old Crown pub – a good place for refreshment.

Go past the pub (keeping it on your right) and turn right on the path by the second house from the pub, The Pink House. It bends round and reaches a field. Go straight down the field and cross a small stream on a footbridge and then over a stile. Bear right across the next

field and cross a very substantial stone slab footbridge. Then go right alongside the small river Ewelme to a stile and continue on through several fields for a good half mile in the same direction with the small river over on your right – not always right next to you. Uley village is up on the right. Reach the beech hedge of a manor house and then the manor walls and go over a stile and onto a path between traditional Cotswold stone and brick walls, passing the entrance to the manor and then on to a road opposite a timeshare development at Stouts Hill.

⑥ Stouts Hill Turn right on the road, and then go left up the 'no through road' to Shadwell Elcombe. Ignore the first footpath on the right, and then by Marsh

Mill House take the next track on the right. Pass a cricket ground and go to the end of the track into the parking area for the house and stable. Take the left-hand of two stiles and bear diagonally down the field, go through a wooden hunting gate and continue on in the same direction to the stream and then bear across and down the field to the stream. Cross a footbridge and go left following the river on your left. Go over a stile by a gate and follow the path which leads onto a track by cottages. Keep straight on by cottages and then right on the track and up to the road.

⑦ Road Turn left, crossing the road onto the pavement and after about a minute, go right on the public footpath,

over a cattle grid on a private farm drive. Stay on the drive, and when it bends left to the farm continue straight on along a grassy track. You pass below Downham Hill up on your right. The track ends at farm buildings. Go straight ahead through a metal gate and then over a stile and head straight down the field end to the far left corner. Ahead is Cam Peak where you were earlier. Go left over a stile and then right and through the farmyard between barns. Reach the farm drive and turn right. Further on just before the next cattle grid take the blue arrowed footpath alongside the farm drive. At the end, turn left on the quiet lane road for about ten minutes to a t-junction, going by several cottages.

Go left towards Dursley past substantial country homes, and shortly, after passing Lansdowne House, go immediately right on the public footpath track. Pass a playing field on the left on the other side of the hedge. Go over a stile and down the right hedge of the field. Cross another stile and fork left down the next field on the outskirts of Upper Cam, heading slightly left of the church. There's another stile and then right in the field and across to a stile on the far side. Now just continue to head for the church until you reach the lane opposite it, near the start of our circle.

Of particular interest are the many table tombs in the churchyard to the Phillimore family and other families connected with the once flourishing cloth and corn mills. Inside the church, the carved Norman font is all that remains of the original 12th Century church.

The Old Crown Inn, at Uley
Tel: 01453 860502

On the level in English parkland

Tetbury – Estcourt Park – Shipton Moyne – Tetbury

6 miles. About 2 hours walking.

OS Explorer map 168, Stroud, Tetbury and Malmesbury

The Cat and Custard Pot is the curiously named village pub at Shipton Moyne, Gloucestershire in the centre of this easy level circle roaming through fields and parkland to the south of Tetbury. The circle takes in the glories of an immaculate old country estate and park on the way to Shipton Moyne and circles back on dry tracks and

lanes. This is equestrian land and the home of the Beaufort Hunt and there will be many horses in the fields on the way round. Near the end we go through a small part of old Tetbury by a ford back to the start – at the old station now converted into an attractive, spacious free car park. It's a very beautiful, memorable walk giving one a real feel of the beauty of this flatter, more open southern part of the Cotswolds.

START at the car park at the **Old Station Yard in Tetbury.** This free long stay car park is well signed and situated to the eastern side of the town on the **Cirencester Road** by the **Royal Oak Pub.** It is between this pub and the **Crown** that the annual gruelling wool sack race takes place up **Gumstool Hill** on the late **May Bank Holiday.** Competitors run with a **60lb** woolsack on their backs. It is a race which was revived in **1973** but dates back to a tradition from the **17th Century** when young men engaged in the wool trade took part in the race in order to show their manliness and impress the ladies! Tetbury's prosperity grew on the back of the wool and yard trade for which it became famous. The town missed out on the Industrial Revolution as the water supply could not cope with growth, this has meant that the sleepy Cotswold town has been left with it's history still standing carved in the wonderful architecture.

1 Old Station Yard This was the terminus for a 75 mile branch single track line from Kemble to Tetbury used mainly for farm feedstuff, livestock, milk and coal. There was a cattle market at the side to contain the livestock.

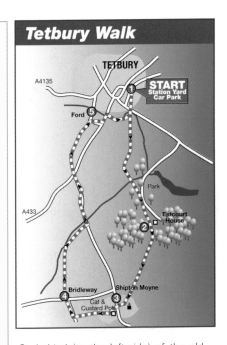

Tetbury Walk

Go behind (to the left side) of the old goods shed and walk along the line of the old railway sleepers which parallel a tarmac path by a stream. Pass a circular decorated brick pavement. This was a communal art project on the site of a crane mounting in the old rail yard. It shows the four points of the compass and each of the hand-made tiles is different. From a meeting I saw was being held in the Autumn of 2004 it seems as though this pavement may be under threat, so don't be surprised if it is no longer here.

Continue along until the path comes up to a road. Cross and take the public footpath opposite. Cross the stream – an embryonic part of the River Avon (Tetbury branch) which rises from a spring nearby in Tetbury – and don't go through the metal gate to the sewage works, but instead take the metal kissing gate on the right of the track. Go through and take the left footpath which goes up, along by a fence and over a stile into a field. Now head along the left edge of the field, gently ascending. It's a beautiful start to the walk with stunning views of the spire of Tetbury church behind you. Soon see an avenue of trees ahead to the right – these are along a grassy drive leading to Estcourt Grange Farm.

Cross a stone slab stile and cross the grassy drive with a bench seat on the right. Continue on hugging the right fence starting to come into park-like countryside. Come to a stile ahead (ignoring hunting gate on the right). Cross the stile and continue for a few more yards along the right fence and then go right through a marked five bar wooden gate. Go down steps and through woodland, over a footbridge over the stream and then over a stile into Estcourt park.

❷ **Estcourt Park** Follow the arrows up across the park. This glorious estate was in the Estcourt family for 700 years – but sadly the old house was burnt down and demolished in 1964. No members of the

© Clint Hughes

Estcourt family live in the area anymore and the estate is run by a Saudi prince as a stud farm. It is beautifully maintained and well signed for walkers.

Continue on, ignoring a drive joining from the right, and continue on to reach gates ahead. Go through and pass the house and buildings on your left staying on the drive. The house on the left is now the office of the estate managment, but was once the Dower House – the home of the Dowager, the mother of the Lord of the Manor. Pass a house on the right and at the end of the wall turn right following the footpath arrow. Cross a stile and follow the arrow going left across a grassy ride,

through a gate and continue across a field. Follow the arrows now across fields, and rides until you start to see rooftops in Shipton Moyne and find yourself going along between railings and a fence. Cross yet another stile and cross over a tarmac drive. Continue straight ahead across the next field and over a stile. On the far

side of this next field is the village and a large farm. Cross diagonally towards the village aiming for the far right corner of the field (passing to the left side of the farm). Cross a stone slab stile and go along a path to come out in the village. You are about one and a half hours into the walk.

❸ Shipton Moyne Go left to the Cat and Custard Pot which was a real bonus when I walked here as it is not marked on the OS map. It is open every day for lunch.

Opposite the pub is a lane leading to St John the Baptist church, an interesting building with a memorial chapel to the Estcourt family.

Take the footpath at the side of the pub. Go over into a field and across. Over a stile and through the next field and cross a stile. In this field. Pass a narrow band of woodland and continue on in the same direction across the field. In the corner cross a stone slab stile and walk through a horse exercise paddock along the right edge. Once over the stile, go through the next field along the right edge to come out on to a lane opposite a magnificent Cotswold house and stud. Turn right and continue to a junction.

Image above and opposite © Clint Hughes

❹ **Bridleway** Cross and take the bridleway opposite. This old route is called Wormwell Lane. Follow it all the way to the end to a lane. Turn left and stay on this quiet lane for about 10 minutes (just over half a mile) until you reach the main A433.

Cross onto the pavement and turn right. Shortly go left on the footpath through a small wood, over a footbridge and out over a stile into a field. Follow the left edge past a line of cobnut trees and

oaks. Tetbury church spire is visible up on the right.

Go left down the side of a barn and into a field and down the right side. In the corner cross a footbridge and pass through a little piece of woodland and over a stile and up into the field. Go across to the far right corner to a stone slab stile.

Turn right on the residential lane and follow this along to a junction. Turn left and start to approach some of the older parts of Tetbury. Go over a bridge by a ford.

❺ **Ford** Immediately turn right on the small lane, pass old cottages and get a stunning view of the church as you climb up and start to near the main road. Cross and turn right along the pavement, making a detour to the church if you wish. After about three minutes go over a stile on a footpath and take the left hand path through a metal kissing gate.

Go through the field and into a wood. Just follow this path which winds through the woodland and then goes under much older trees. Come down to a stile you crossed earlier. Go left over the stile, left through a kissing gate and retrace your steps up the track. Cross the main

© Clint Hughes

road and make your way back to the old
station yard.

The Cat and Custard Pot,
Shipton Moyne,
 Tel: 01666 880249

Hawkesbury: a Cotswold haven

Hawkesbury Upton – Lower Kilcott – Hawkesbury – Hawkesbury Upton

5 miles. 2.45 hours walking.

OS Explorer map 167, Thornbury, Dursley and Yate, ref: 775869

This very unspoilt and tranquil rolling area to the west of the Badminton estate is typical Cotswold combe country, ideal for quiet walking surrounded by woods, curvaceous grassy slopes and changing views. It's an easy circle from Hawkesbury Upton on the south west fringes of the Cotswolds, ideal for a morning, finishing with lunch at one of the two pubs in the village. Spring brings this area to its full glory with swathes of wild garlic, bluebells and wood anemones. We pass glorious mellow cottages, the charming and historic hamlet of Hawkesbury and the Somerset Monument. There are a couple of slight uphills en route and a steeper climb near the end.

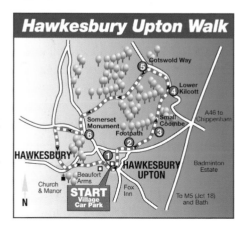

❶ Village car park Go along the High Street (left if coming from the car park) passing the Beaufort Arms and reach the Fox Inn. Take the footpath on the far side of the pub. Go through the pub garden and over a stile and straight ahead following the left wall. Cross a stile into another field and go ahead, with views over on the left to the Somerset monument which we visit later. Go over a stile down on the far side onto a lane and turn right for a few minutes.

❷ Footpath Opposite a lane on the right, go left on the marked footpath which drops gently downhill. Cross a stile and carry on gradually descending and bearing away from the right fence into a tranquil valley. Cross a stile by a gate and continue on down the next field, as before, over another stile by a gate and on down the third field. Cross a stile on the far side situated to the right of a gate, go ahead a few yards and then left through a gate into the field at the side and go straight on down. Cross a small footbridge over the stream that runs through this valley, known as Upton Coombe. Turn right following the stream on your right.

❸ **Small Coombe** Cross a stile and enter Small Coombe, continuing along the grassy swathe by the stream in this pretty sheltered valley which can be very sunny. The sides were studded with primroses when I came here with the promise of much garlic and bluebells. For about half a mile continue to follow the stream in the open area between woodland ignoring side tracks to the left and later a track going up right. Eventually reach a gate onto a lane at Lower Kilcott (unmarked).

❹ **Lower Kilcott** Turn left on this quiet little lane for just under half a mile, passing beautiful stone houses and reaching the marked bridleway on the left, the Cotswold Way.

❺ **Cotswold Way** Go uphill on the sunken track, forking left still climbing. Cross a stile by a gate and follow the bridleway arrow right and then left up the edge of the field with a sunken track down on left and pretty Long Coombe down on the right. Cross a stile by a gate and go through woodland. When the track becomes smaller near a gate on the left, it can become muddy but a parallel, drier path has been created to the right. It's easy to find. The two rejoin later by a gate on the left with a stile.

Cross the stile into the field on the left and go right paralleling woodland over on the right. Head towards a barn ahead. Soon see the Somerset Monument up on the left. Reach a hedge corner sticking into the field and continue on now following the hedge on your right. Carry on across to the road. Turn left on the road for a few minutes uphill.

❻ **Somerset Monument** This imposing monument commemorates one of the Duke of Beaufort's sons General Lord Robert Edward Henry Somerset

© Clint Hughes

who fought with Wellington and died at Waterloo. It was built in 1846 on the highest point in the area which used to be the village bowls green. It used to be possible to climb its 144 steps and enjoy views of the River Severn, the Forest of Dean, Welsh mountains and the Bristol Channel. It is recorded that when Queen Mary visited the monument in World War Two, the caretaker did not recognise her and asked one of her attendants for the 2 pence fee to ascend the monument. Queen Mary had no money to hand but her equerry produced a pound!

Take the lane on the right marked to Wickwar and follow this quiet route downhill for about five minutes. Opposite a lane which comes in on the right, go left through a gate onto a track. Follow it along passing up on the left Hawkesbury Knoll long barrow. The track comes to the pretty hamlet of Hawkesbury. Take the gate to the right of the cottage and come out onto the lane.

❼ Hawkesbury This picturesque hamlet has a history of settlement going back to Neolithic times. Life for centuries revolved around the church and manor and its wealth was founded on the wool trade like many local villages where there was plenty of natural water. If you are fortunate the church of St Mary's may be open, and it is well worth a visit. Turn left on the lane passing the church and soon go up right on the marked footpath. This is the steepest section up through woodland and over a stile at the top into a field. Ignore any green 'environmentally sensitive' arrows which may be in evidence. Just cross the narrow strip of field and go through the hedge opposite into a field. Head up to the top left corner with good views as you go across left to the monument. Cross a stile and follow the left hedge in this field. A stile brings you onto a crossing track, Bath Lane, an old Roman route. Cross into the field opposite and follow the left hedge all the way back to Hawkesbury Upton.

Beaufort Arms
Tel: 01454 238217
Book in advance and park at the pub, go in any time from 9.30am and order your meal to be ready when you return.

Fox Inn
Tel: 01454 238219.
The same applies here. Let them know you are coming and will be having lunch and you can use the car park.

Ramble round Badminton

Luckington − Great Badminton − Little Badminton
− Luckington

5.75 miles. 3 hours walking.

OS Explorer map 168, Stroud, Tetbury & Malmesbury, ref: 31 840

This circle is in the heart of equestrian Cotswold country with riders out and about, horses grazing in paddocks and fields, cross country horse jumps and on top of this the chance to see the beautiful estate village of Badminton and the park which is the venue for the Badminton Trials venue. Pretty Luckington village is where you start and finish and it is here that you can enjoy refreshment at the renowned pub. The circle passes an ancient burial mound and the pretty hamlet of Little Badminton with an ancient Dovecote. The walk can be shortened but the full version of nine miles takes you up to the pretty village of Didmarton and a welcoming inn. If you choose to do this walk on any of the four days of the Horse Trials you will not be allowed in the park, unless you pay the entry, so you will have to walk round the road, about 15 miles. Walking is more or less flat on quiet dry tracks, bridleways and lanes.

START **Park somewhere suitable in the village of Luckington which is on the B4040 road between Acton Turville and Malmesbury. It is easily reached from junctions 17 or 18 of the M4.**

❶ Post Office Go to the post office stores on the main road. Cross over and follow the public footpath up steps to the right of a yellow hydrant. At the end of the path cross a stile and bear over left and ahead to a marked opening into a field. Head across the field bearing slightly left to a gate on the far side (no footpath sign here). Go through and then follow the right hedge down to the bottom. Cross a stone slab stile, waymarked, onto a lane and turn left.

Pass a farm on the right and at a bend in the road, go left into the field following the footpath sign. Head down and across the field in the direction of the bottom far corner and go through a marked gate some way before the corner on the far side. Head diagonally left down this next field to the bottom corner. Go out onto the lane and turn left. Shortly where the next field ends on the left you will see on the left a tree covered mound.

❷ Giants Cave Also known as Luckington Long Barrow, it is multi chambered and one of only two remaining in the West Country. There were eight chambers but several were destroyed when the road was built. It's dilapidated and covered in trees, but the

© Clint Hughes

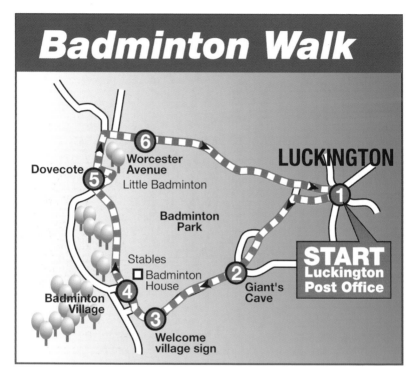

Badminton Walk

Dovecote
Worcester Avenue
Little Badminton
6
5
LUCKINGTON
1
Badminton Park
Stables
☐ Badminton House
2
Giant's Cave
START
Luckington Post Office
Badminton Village
4
3
Welcome village sign

stones of the side chambers still poke out of the earth. Apparently there used to be 'an old boy' in the village who kept a skull 'for a momento'.

Continue on down the road and at the junction turn right on the lane to Badminton.

This runs along one side of Badminton Park. You get a good view of Badminton House, the home of the Dukes of Beaufort, and it is here that stands and arenas are set up for the Trials. In medieval times the park would have been used for hunting deer and hare as well as the raising of horses.

❸ Welcome village sign Pass the 'Welcome to Badminton' sign and just before the bend go right through a hunting gate and follow a small path along with the park on the right. This is the Duchess's Walk and I am assured that sensible

walkers will be welcomed. (If you find the way barred then carry on along the lane a little further and turn right and carry on into Badminton village). Follow the path giving beautiful views of the House and reach the drive. Turn left through the entrance gate and into the village.

❹ Badminton Village Go right (or straight across if coming from the lane) on the Private Road No Entry marked with a public footpath sign. Follow this past stables and estate buildings. Cross a bridge and come into the Park. Follow the tarmac drive straight ahead through what will be the centre of activity during the Trials. Pass

a lake over on the right and take the left fork. This tarmac drive continues through the Park and soon you will start to see the village of Little Badminton in the distance. Go out through park gates.

❺ Dovecote Opposite is a medieval Dovecote, one of the best in the county.

© Clint Hughes

It is the only remaining building from the medieval village which is now buried below the surface.

Turn right down the small lane which bends round through the pretty and secluded settlement of Little Badminton. Pass the pretty Early English church, sadly locked, and reach the road again. Turn right.

Pass the derestriction sign and then woodland on your right. At the end of the woodland, turn right on the marked public footpath which is a tarmac lane at this point. At the left bend, follow the track ahead. Reach a wide crossing grassy drive, Worcester Avenue.

⑥ Worcester Avenue This was one of the entrance drives to Badminton House. Just follow the track straight ahead all the way to a hunting gate and reach a hard-core track. Continue on and the

© Clint Hughes

track becomes a Tarmac lane. Pass a
stone barn, Lippiatt Barn, and continue
on into Cherry Orchard Lane which leads
on back to Luckington.

The Old Royal Ship
Luckington
Tel: 01666 840222

Follow the old mill stream

Castle Combe – Ford – Castle Combe

5.6 miles, about 2.75 hours walking.

OS Explorer Map 156, Chippenham and Bradford on Avon, ref 845 777

One of England's most picturesque villages is at the heart of this very southern Cotswold circle. It is a mixture of uphill and downdale, through tranquil, idyllic combe country following a clear trout stream, once a powerful mill stream powering the wool industry. We stop at a renowned waterside16th Century inn and then go through a lightly grazed area, designated as a Site of Special Scientific Interest and enjoy beautiful Cotswold stone cottages and the pretty market cross at the heart of Castle Combe.

© Clint Hughes

START at the large free car park in Upper Castle Combe. It is well signed and is just off the B4039 Chipping Sodbury – Chippenham road to the north of the village.

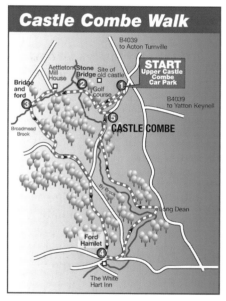

Castle Combe Walk

❶ **Car Park** Take the steps from the car park to the road and turn right. Fork right after two minutes at the junction and start to descend towards the village. Almost immediately, bear right on a drive which goes up ahead and passes in front of what was once three tenements built for workers in the wool industry. The other house on the right is the old school.

Take the footpath ahead – this first stretch is not always well maintained (ignoring the wider cycle path on the right) and find yourself alongside Manor House golf course. It is situated on the site of a 13th Century castle and an earlier ancient British camp. Stay over to the left, hugging the wall. Carry on descending gently and ignore a stile and steps on the left. (We return over this stile). Just continue along the wall on the marked path. Eventually run alongside a tarmac drive on the golf course and then join it, turning right.

❷ **Stone bridge** Cross the bridge over the By Brook, still on the tarmac path. The Brook was the reason for the growth of Castle Combe. It provided the power to drive corn, and for fulling and gig mills. At the height of the wool industry in the 15th Century, there were 132 mills operating along the By Brook, creating fortunes for the clothiers. The red and white cloth produced was much sought after on the continent where it was known as 'castlecombe' and was also worn as a uniform by men at arms of Sir Joon Fastolf, the then Baron. It is thought that Shakespeare based the character of Falstaff in Henry IV on Sir John Fastolf of Castle Combe.

Just before another bridge and a wooden rail on the left, go left off the drive on the Macmillan Way footpath and follow this, with the stream down on your right. Keep on all the way to a wall with a kissing gate set in it, at converted Nettleton mill house. Go through the gate and ahead up the drive for a few yards and turn left between buildings. It is not marked but it is a clear path taking you along with the stream now over on your left. Follow it all the way along to a junction with another path.

❸ **Bridge and ford** Turn left and cross an old stone clapper bridge over the Broadmead Brook alongside a ford.

© Clint Hughes

© Clint Hughes

Follow the track up out of the valley, quite steep at first. The track drops downhill to a lane.

Turn left and follow this quiet thoroughfare. Reach a junction with the Castle Combe lane coming in from the left. Go ahead a couple of yards on the Ford road and then go right through a metal gate and follow the marked footpath to Ford left through woodland. You are now about 80 minutes from the start. Enter a field on the path and follow it all the way along, dropping gently down and then it drops more steeply down through a wood and coming into another field. Again go along the length of this field.

Drop down to a bridge over the stream and continue ahead through a long narrow field and just near the end of the field the path bears up right and then continues on in the same direction as before under trees. Go through another open area and reach a timber clad stone house on the left and go left through the keyhole stile. Follow the stony track out to the main road in Ford.

❹ **Ford hamlet** Our walk continues by going left along the main road for a very short distance. But the pub is only a detour of a couple of minutes: For the pub, go right a few yards and then cross and take the lane opposite down to the White Hart, a 16th Century inn and hotel, beautifully situated by the water, with an attractive riverside terrace.

Continue on the main road and take the first turn left on the Castle Combe road. It climbs quite steeply uphill. On the bend at the top go right over a stile on the footpath marked to Long Dean.

Go through the open field on the path. Reach a metal gate on the edge of woodland. Go through and carry on under trees on this path fringed with harts tongue ferns. The path takes you to the hamlet of Long Dean with a converted mill house and other glorious old stone houses by the stream.

At a footpath sign by a post box in the wall, go left. The tarmac drive becomes rougher but just continue on. It is well marked and takes you along through woodland, over stiles and into an Area of Special Scientific Interest and into a high open field with good views down over the combe. In the field, ignore the right fork. Stay over to the left and the path takes you down to the By Brook again over a stone bridge and to the road on the edge of Castle Combe.

Turn right into the village, passing toilets on your left, and enjoying the picturesque old weavers cottages.

❺ Castle Combe At the 14th Century market cross, turn left. Here, St Andrew's church is well worth a visit. The church was extensively restored in the 19th Century but much of the old work remains. Round the top of the tower run 76 arches high and low. The parapet is carved with nearly fifty stone heads. Looking down on the roof is a carving of a shuttle and scissors the mark of the cloth industry put there by the wool merchants who built the tower.

The Jesse East window of Victorian glass is memorable and it is interesting to see the roof timbers, which are resting on carved stone heads depicting the lords of the manor, the priest, the mason and the folk who began the life of the church. A notable feature is the early clock brought down from the tower in 1984 and in working order just below the tower. There is also a superb stone monument dated 1270, made by Bristol craftsmen, of Walter de Dunstanville, Baron of Castle Combe, with his six children below him, weeping.

To continue go, past the entrance to Manor House Hotel – an extension and conversion of the original Castle Combe Manor House – and under an arch and follow the track round a bend, climbing out of the village. Reach a wall and stile

where you were earlier. Turn right and retrace your steps along the wall, along the edge of the golf course, staying over to the right and picking up a path through rough lane to the lane by the old school and cottages. At the main road, turn left and shortly, left again back up to the car park.

The White Hart, Ford
Tel: 01249 782213